FAREWELL, ALEPPO

CLAUDETTE E. SUTTON

FAREWELL, ALEPPO

*My Father, My People, and Their
Long Journey Home*

Terra Nova Books

SANTA FE, NEW MEXICO

Distributed by SCB Distributors, (800) 729-6423

Terra Nova Books

Published by Terra Nova Books, Santa Fe, New Mexico.
www.TerraNovaBooks.com

ISBN 978-1-938288-40-1

Acknowledgments

Many people read this book along the way and offered invaluable suggestions and wisdom. Special thanks to Adam Beyda, Charles Brunn, Ariel Brunn, Robert Sutton, Lynn Hathaway, Elaine Pinkerton Coleman, Jennet Grover, Cinny Green, David Brightman, Rachel O'Keefe, Carole Cristiano, Nina Bunker Ruiz, Ken Terry, Denise Betesh, Ellen Zieselman, Rosemary Zibart, Mary Beyda, Abraham Marcus, and Marsha Heller.

A posse of friends and family members contributed to my research and writing; my heartfelt gratitude to Elie Sutton, Ralph Sutton, Joe Sutton, Eileen Sutton, Robert Sutton, Kathleen Sutton, Vivian Beyda and Irving Beyda, and other family members for sharing memories, photos, and encouragement; and to Gail and Martin Tierney for graciously providing a sunny place to write and let this project percolate.

Thanks to Terra Nova Books: Scott Gerber, publisher and designer, who went above and beyond the beyond; and Marty Gerber, editor, mentor, and friend.

Art Tucker, of Artotems Co., reminded me to "Smile! You're on Social Media!"

A lifetime of thanks to my grandparents: Selim Sutton, for holding the dream; Adele Sutton, whose courage, strength, and sacrifice I hope I have honored; and Esther and Abraham Beyda, who contributed to these pages with a bequest of love, joy, family, home, and the world's greatest foods: Your legacies live on.

Over the moon thanks to my dad, Mike Sutton, who shared his life so trustingly, and my mama, Cynthia Sutton, who shared her husband so patiently. I love you both more than words can say.

Lastly, not leastly, thanks to Ariel, my sun and moon, and Charles, my star.

For the grandchildren

Contents

Foreword

n my first trip to Israel, I was surprised to discover that there was no lox, bagels, or cream cheese served at breakfast.

For my family of origin from the Eastern European Pale of Settlement, those were the essential elements of breakfast. Eventually during the year I lived in Jerusalem, I came to understand that my Sephardic friends (in this case from the Kurdistan area of Iran) had never eaten smoked salmon or bagels. Instead, I came to appreciate *shakshouka* (eggs in tomato sauce) for breakfast, and for dinner *kibbeh b'marak* (ground meat stuffed in sort of a dumpling, served in soup). A lot of work to make, but oh so delicious! Like the music and other traditions, the food and the way they served it was different. But the people were warm, loving, open, and welcoming.

The range of Jewish cultures I saw in Israel in that time is an essential part of Claudette Sutton's story of her father and family, based on her expertise as both an interviewer and a researcher. But the book she gives us here is a compelling human tale in addition to a historic one—from her grandfather's fraught decision to "export" his sons, to her father's journey across continents and oceans, to the uniqueness of this special segment of American immigrant culture.

As I have come to understand in my study of Jewish history, and as the family of Selim Sutton personifies, we are a people "scattered among the nations." In my own world, I look back now on my travels and relish the thought that I have met Jews in and from dozens of countries around the world.

Yet for all of that, I never expected to have a Syrian Jew—

On my first trip to Israel, I was surprised to discover that there was no lox, bagels, and cream cheese served at breakfast.

the author of this book—in my congregation. And the idea of a Jewish Syrian diaspora just never entered my mind. What a great pity! We do such violence to the richness and diversity of a people's heritage around the world, and in particular in America, if we lock them out of our awareness.

Beyond the importance of culture that Claudette Sutton makes so clear, there are also the elements of education—a key to not just survival but thriving—and the sense of family deeply ingrained in the psyche. The story of the unique individuals she writes about is painted both in personal terms and with broad strokes on the canvas of history across a timeframe of extraordinary circumstance. Machines replacing the era of horses, a world swept into the consuming fires of war, the dawn of the nuclear age—who could imagine such drama, such jeopardy, such sweeping changes in the world of human endeavor?

How was it that a merchant in Aleppo would be prescient enough to foresee that after generations as Jewish Syrians, his family would have to leave behind everything familiar?

How was it that a merchant in Aleppo would be prescient enough to foresee that after generations as Jewish Syrians, his family would have to leave behind everything familiar because the country and culture he had known was about to end? Somehow, he knew. Perhaps something in his upbringing opened him up to the possibilities of a new future. Certainly strength of will, and of character, were essential to make possible his difficult and painful decisions. Continued survival is not for the faint of heart.

So as you read this book, accept the invitation to come into the welcoming precincts of a culture where the richness of expression is found not in Yiddish but in Ladino and even Arabic. Immerse yourself in the story of a fascinating individual—Mike Sutton—as he leaves a life shaped by faith and time for one he builds in a new land through his own personal character and strength. Open yourself up to a part of a people's rich heritage as vibrant and caring as anything you could imagine—and enjoy the journey!

—Rabbi Marvin Schwab,
Temple Beth Shalom,
Santa Fe, New Mexico

INTRODUCTION
Adele's Token

pen the light," my grandmother said. The front door of her Brooklyn house was ajar on that Friday evening in mid-September, just after dusk, but the house was dark.

I had not been in my grandmother's house since I was a little girl. Back then, she lived on the ground floor of a brick

My grandmother, Adele Sutton, on the steps of the family's last home in Aleppo, 1946.

Grandma Sutton's house in Brooklyn, 2014.

duplex. I remember being intrigued on a family visit by the two side-by-side front doors—one opening to my grand-mother's home on the ground floor, the other leading upstairs to the apartment where my father's brother Morris lived with his wife, Frieda. I remember my grandmother's kitchen and living room crammed with people in fancy clothes. Adele Sutton, my father's mother, had come to New York from Aleppo, Syria, not long before I was born, and spoke halting English.

On a long-ago day, after everyone had been fed, she put a hand on my little arm and led me to her bedroom, opened an inlaid wooden jewelry box, took out a tiny stickpin with a gold heart at the end, and pinned it to my blouse.

When I entered college in the fall of 1980, she lived just across the street from the house I had visited as a little girl, in another brick house with Morris, Frieda, and their children. I had just moved to New York from Maryland to enroll at the New School in Lower Manhattan. When the battery was stolen from my car parked near my Manhattan apartment, I arranged with my grandmother to keep my car at her house for a few months until I could drive it back to my parents' home in Maryland. Finding my way through the residential streets of Flatbush to her house in the heart of Brooklyn's massive Syrian-Jewish community, I could hear her voice in my head reciting directions over the phone in a thick Arabic accent.

The neighborhood's narrow, tree-lined streets seemed quiet and chilly that evening compared with Manhattan's everyday chaos. Going there to leave off my car, I found the house and pulled in the driveway as Frieda came out in a thick blue bathrobe and pointed me to the garage. I remember her first brusque words to the niece she had never met: "Lock it." I did as she said and walked around to the front of the house as Frieda bolted the garage shut.

"Hello?" I said as I pushed open the door, smiling nervously. "Where are you? It's dark in here!"

My tiny grandmother, even shorter than I am, rose from a couch by the window. "Open the light," she said, pointing to a switch. She gave me both hands, and I squeezed the soft, loose skin of her hands as I leaned down to kiss her cheek.

"Sit," she said, gesturing to one of the lush sofas that lined the opposite walls, leaving a large bare space in the middle of the room. The room had a just-cleaned look that I somehow knew it always had.

"You're skin," she said.

"Skinny?"

"Yes," she answered. I shrugged. All my life, Jewish grandmothers had been telling me I was too thin. Frieda came in from the garage and sat on the sofa next to her mother-in-law, translating for us occasionally between Arabic and English.

"How long are you here?" Frieda asked in a New York syntax I had not yet deciphered.

"Oh, I don't know how long I'll be here," I said. From her puzzled look, I realized she wanted to know when I'd arrived. "But I got here about a month ago," I added. She asked if I would spend the night, but I had to decline. I had class early the next morning, a Saturday. My grandmother grumbled in Arabic.

> My tiny grandmother, even shorter than I am, rose from a couch by the window. "Open the light," she said, pointing to a switch.

"You'll eat?" Grandma Sutton asked.

"Of course," I said with a conciliatory smile—due compensation to her in my mind for not staying the night.

I followed my grandmother and Aunt Frieda through the dining room to the bright yellow kitchen where an overhead light had been left on and took a seat at the little table. Morris and the boys were at the synagogue, Frieda explained, and would eat when they came home. My grandmother brought plate after plate from the refrigerator, trip after trip, long after I assumed she had finished, until I had salad, rice, bean soup, pickles, olives, bread, bean salad, and a few Syrian pastries in front of me. "Eat," she commanded.

> I felt Frieda's wide eyes assessing me as I ate alone. I was part of her family after all—the youngest daughter of her husband's oldest brother, first cousin to her children—yet I'd grown up far from this large Syrian-Jewish community.

Frieda sat opposite me, pushing her frizzy black hair off her forehead. I felt her wide eyes assessing me as I ate alone. I was part of her family after all—the youngest daughter of her husband's oldest brother, first cousin to her children— yet I'd grown up far from this large Syrian-Jewish community. Shortly after they married, my parents had moved to Maryland, where my brother and sister and I were raised near my maternal grandparents. They were also Syrian but lived much-more-assimilated American lives. We visited our Brooklyn relatives only rarely and did not observe Orthodox Jewish rules or keep kosher, as they all did. (I remember my anxiety as a child staying overnight at the home of one of my New York cousins, wondering how long I should wait after the meat-based dinner before asking for a glass of milk. I didn't want them to know I didn't know.) Watching my grandmother study me, I realized why she had asked me to turn on the light. She knew I would not refrain from using a light switch on the Sabbath, as the Orthodox did.

Frieda plied me with questions. "Is everyone in your family vegetarian?"—as I was at the time. "Which do you like better, Washington or New York?" "Where do you buy your clothes, New York or Washington?" (I dared not mention that most of my clothes came from thrift stores and yard sales. My Brooklyn relatives observe the most ancient Jewish traditions, but most of them also sport the most up-to-the-

minute fashions.) I realized that Manhattan—which Frieda
simply called New York—was a world apart from Brooklyn,
one that she and my grandmother rarely visited.

My grandfather,
Selim Sutton, and
grandmother,
Adele Laniado
Sutton, in
Aleppo, 1948.

My grandmother asked about my parents and siblings, the
baby my sister was expecting that fall, then went back to the
living room. When I had eaten as much as I could hold, end-
ing with a luscious, sticky wedge of baklava, she returned to
the kitchen, huffing with disappointment that I had not had
more. Wouldn't I stay the night, she asked again, concerned
about my taking the subway alone after dark. I repeated that
I wished I could stay but needed to go to my morning class.
She huffed again. Frieda would walk me to the station.

While Frieda dressed, I surveyed the photos in the living
room. There were wedding photos of all my grandmother's
children, including my father as a dapper young man with a
tuxedo and reticent smile, and groups of grandchildren pos-
ing next to a tree or in front of a house. Frieda walked with
me the few blocks to the subway in a light drizzle, pulling a
plastic rain hat over her head, concerned that the rain would
frizz her hair even more. I held an umbrella from my grand-

My parents'
wedding, 1950.

mother over us, and passed it off to Frieda at the subway.

A few weeks later, I went back to my grandmother's house for the big Syrian feast she made for her family every Sunday. I arrived early and helped her arrange the little plates of Syrian food on the long dining room table—*mwada* (triangles of filo dough filled with spinach, cheese, and egg), *ka'ak* (crispy cracker-rings topped with sesame seeds), *sambusac* (crescent-shaped pastries filled with cheese and egg), nuts, olives, pickles, tahini, string cheese, bean and vegetable salads, neatly cut triangles of Syrian bread, and tiny pastries in various shapes drizzled with sweet syrup.

I stood beside my little grandmother as she scrutinized the table for a final check. "There's not enough," I said under my breath with mock gravity. Her eyes darted up at me, flashing anxiety until she saw my jesting smile. She laughed, swatting me lightly with her hand, a row of gold bracelets jingling on her wrist.

Soon the large open space in the living room filled with children whose family resemblance I could not mistake but whose names I didn't know. My father is the oldest of my grandmother's eight children. He had come to America and started a family years before any of his brothers, so I was older than most of these cousins, many of whom I'd never met. Syrian-Jewish tradition sets specific rules for naming children: First-born sons are named after their father's father; first daughters after their father's mother; the next boy and girl for the maternal grandparents. Four of my father's brothers, Elie, Ralph, Joe, and Morris, were in the house that day, each with their eldest sons named for Samuel, as their paternal grandfather Selim's name was Americanized when the family arrived in America. Adults distinguished one child from another by tacking on the father's name as a suffix, so all afternoon I heard calls to "Sammy-Joe!" "Sammy-Ralph!" "Sammy-Morris!" "Sammy-Elie!"

"Eat!" my Auntie Tunie, Elie's wife, teased me. "It's ethnic food!" This saddened me. I wanted it to be *my* food, to be a fully integrated member of this family since I was, after all, a full-blooded constituent. I wanted to know the names of these beautiful children with their playful, intelligent eyes, to be their familiar older cousin, not a benevolent stranger. Yet I knew *I* was the ethnic one here, the cultural hybrid, a cross between our shared heritage and my secular upbringing. I was a purebred member of this community, and a visitor to it.

The two hundred miles between Maryland and New York belied the chasm between my cousins' upbringing and my own. My Brooklyn relatives observed Orthodox Jewish rituals of praying, eating, fasting, wedding, mourning, and dying, as our ancestors had for centuries in Aleppo. My mother came from the same background. Her father, Abraham Beyda, had come to America from Aleppo with his family at the turn of the last century. My mother's mother, Esther Bijou, was born in Cairo, but her father had moved from Syria for business opportunities not long before my grandmother's birth. These grandparents had lived in Brooklyn for a few years after they married, then moved to Washington, D.C., during the Depression.

Soon the large open space in the living room filled with children whose family resemblance I could not mistake but whose names I didn't know.

In our little Syrian enclave in the Maryland suburbs, my siblings, cousins, and I enjoyed many of the traditional foods and customs, as we drifted further into the mainstream. By the time I entered college, living in a scrappy East Village apartment with my cat, Pekoe, I was far too entrenched in my American independence to blend seamlessly into the Brooklyn Syrian community, where girls married as teens, boys went into their fathers' businesses, and first cousins shared first names. Their clannishness felt alien to me, while I nevertheless envied the closeness that they took for granted. When a community member gets sick or a relative dies, a posse comes forth to offer support. Women gather in one another's kitchens to prepare the *kibbehs* and other labor-intensive foods for Friday night dinners. They vacation *en masse* every summer to the same beach town, Deal, New Jersey. If there is little room for individuality, there is equally little room for loneliness.

My grandmother gave me a subway token for my return trip to Manhattan, but it was an old one that no longer worked. I kept it for years.

With my Grandmother Adele, I had few common words and fewer shared experiences. Instead, I offered my presence, smiles, affection, and a little jesting. Before I left that Sunday afternoon, she gave me bags of food to take home and a token for the subway. It was an old one, issued before the most recent fare increase, and no longer worked in the turnstiles. I bought a new one at the station and tucked hers into my pocket. I kept it for years.

The Word for Morning

hen I was a little girl, growing up in Maryland, my father owned a children's clothing store on F Street in Washington, D.C., in what was then the city's main downtown shopping district. A couple of times each year, he would take the train to New York on buying trips for the next season. Dad would meet with clothing manufacturers in Manhattan for a few days and often spend the night at his mother's house in the far reaches of Brooklyn.

I can still feel the excitement of hearing the front door open after one of those trips. I can feel the soft, carpeted stairs under my little feet as I ran down from my bedroom to greet

my dad after what seemed like a long absence. "What'd you bring me?" I would ask, tugging at his pants, waiting for him to lift me up into his arms. And I can still hear his customary, soft-spoken reply: "Only me."

I came to think of that as my father's opening line in the theater of our home. "Who's that?" Mom would call out from the kitchen when she heard the door open as Dad came home from work or a tennis game.

"Only me," he would reply, with his trace of an Arabic accent. (Only years later did I learn that this was a little joke

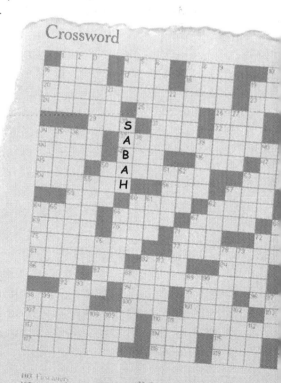

My dad's parents and brothers in Aleppo. Top row, from left, Grandfather Selim, Saleh, and Grandmother Adele. Middle row, Joe, Ralph, and Morris. Front row, Edgar, 1946.

between him and my mother, apparently from a line in an old radio program: "It's only me, Mr. Slovotkin.")

Dad has always been what I would call a soft sell, an under-dramatizer. My mother is quicker to rush into a conversation, finishing her husband's sentences and chiming in from the background on his phone calls. Though I would never have described him as "only Dad," I took for granted that I knew most of what there was to know about this man who went to work in a hat and topcoat, and came home in time to watch Walter Cronkite with a glass of Scotch before we all sat down to dinner.

Shortly after I moved to New York to go to college, I went home for Thanksgiving with my family. I sprawled on my parents' bed that morning, doing the *New York Times* cross-word puzzle as the Macy's parade played on TV, grateful to see my overwhelming new city reduced to the dimensions of a television screen. Dad read the newspaper in the armchair beside the bed, while Mom was in her bathroom getting dressed. I almost gave up on that Thursday's difficult puzzle when Dad, another crossword buff, asked if I needed help.

"Thanks," I said, adding—rhetorically, of course—"but who would know the Turkish word for 'morning'?"

"*Sabah*," he said. I wrote the letters in the squares.

In some foggy corner of my brain, I remembered hearing that Dad had lived in Turkey as a child, although I could not have said at what age or in what circumstances. For whatever reason—perhaps modesty, perhaps the habit of silence that grows in people who spend many years away from those with whom they shared early experiences—my father had never talked much about growing up in Syria, or living in Turkey, or spending the war years in China before coming to America. What I knew about his life I had gleaned in disconnected bits, and I assumed I knew more or less how they fit together. Then one Thanksgiving morning, he tossed me the Turkish word for morning, and I wondered: How much more don't I know about this man, my father?

$$\text{\Large ☙}$$

Living in Maryland, keeping a non-kosher home, my family nonetheless had a traditional Syrian Friday night dinner almost every week: *hamud* (a tangy soup/sauce of vegetables, lemon, garlic, and mint served over rice), roast chicken and potatoes, vegetables stuffed with meat and onions. We gath-

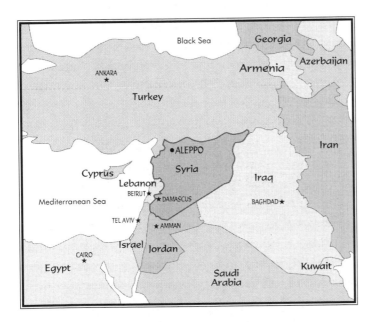

Today's boundaries of Syria and its neighbors. Aleppo is located on a high desert plain in the northern region, about 30 miles from Turkey.

The modern-day country of Syria, in fact, scarcely ever earned mention in our homes, and when it did, the country on the TV news, perhaps embroiled in battle with Israel, seemed far removed from the one my relatives had left a generation before.

ered with our cousins at our grandmother's house nearly every Sunday, the enticing aromas of fried *kibbehs* and *sambusac* greeting us even as we walked up the steps to the front door. My father and grandfather recited Hebrew prayers at home on holidays with traditional Syrian intonation—smokier and more ethereal than the versions we heard in our synagogue with members primarily of Ashkenazi descent, from Germany, Eastern Europe, or Russia. Even today, my siblings, cousins, and I cook many of the same delicious and evocative dishes in our own kitchens that our grandmother made on those Sunday afternoons and holidays.

Whatever this impassioned allegiance is focused on, it is not the land of Syria itself. Throughout my childhood, I never picked up even a hint of nostalgia for a Syrian "motherland." No Aleppoan "Tara" hovered in the family consciousness; no lips uttered, "Next year in Syria" at the Passover seder. Unlike so many immigrant groups, my relatives seemed to harbor not even remote fantasies of returning to the mythic "Old Country," even for a visit.

The modern-day country of Syria, in fact, scarcely ever earned mention in our homes, and when it did, the country on the TV news, perhaps embroiled in battle with Israel, seemed far removed from the one my relatives had left a generation before. To my eyes, it seemed that *their* Syria had not so much been left behind as relocated—to Brooklyn. Our identification as Syrian Jews seemed defined not so much by place as by the culture they took with them.

My door to that "something else" opened several years ago when my father asked me to help him write of his experience growing up in Syria and coming to America. By then, I was living in Santa Fe, New Mexico, with my husband and young son, editing a quarterly newspaper for families and doing other writing as well.

"People have been asking me about my life, how I got to America," Dad said. "I'd like you to help me get my story down on paper." It was a casual, seemingly easy, request. Honored and curious, of course I agreed.

On my next visit to my parents' house in Maryland, I sat down with my father in his basement office, the former guest bedroom where my siblings and I had had sleepovers and parties as kids. I came with a mini-recorder and a list of questions. Dad, in his early 70s then, sat behind his big desk, surrounded by photos of his children and grandchildren. On the wall behind him hung pictures of his brothers and himself at family weddings and bar mitzvahs—smartly dressed men with high, broad foreheads and wide, confident smiles.

"I'd like you to help me get my story down on paper," Dad said. It was a casual, seemingly easy, request. Honored and curious, of course I agreed.

I remember Dad's first, tentative words as I hit the start button: "This is the life story of me—Mike Sutton!"

As I fiddled with the photo cube of his grandchildren on his desk, formulating my next question and the next, I felt as if someone had opened the door of a vault. In the capricious sequences commanded by memory, Dad unwrapped stories from tissue paper where they'd been squirreled away for years. I smile now as I think of families in which a parent or uncle launches a story of life in the old days and eyes roll in silent protestation: *Oh, not that one again!* With my father, it was just the opposite.

"Dad," I blurted out as the tape recorder rolled. "Do you realize how interesting this is? This is our family treasure."

"Is it really?" he asked, his thick white eyebrows rising up his forehead. Yes, it was. How could I have known that his mother bought milk from the farmer who walked his dairy cow down the street in front of their house in Aleppo on his way to market; or that his father traveled to Turkey and Europe buying textiles to sell at home; or that he and one of his brothers had sailed from Egypt to Shanghai on their own as teens, finding it a route to get to America; or that he would be stranded in China alone throughout World War II, selling sewing needles to survive, or that . . . .

My father's simple request launched myriad questions in my own mind about identity, family, and culture; what remains, what evolves, and what is left behind.

From those first conversations in the basement, almost twenty years and many thousands of hours of interviews ago, I learned as much as I could about my father, our Syrian heritage, the land where our Jewish ancestors had lived for millennia and now can no longer live safely—and a way of life forever changed but too precious to forget. For historical context, I turned to books, films, photos, and the Internet, discovering a country a million times more fascinating than I could have imagined, with Jewish culture not merely stitched superfluously on top but woven into its very fibers. We no longer have family members in Aleppo—a peculiar blessing today given the country's violence and chaos—yet so far-reaching is Syria's influence on its Jewish descendants that generations who have never been inside Syrian borders continue to define themselves as Syrian Jews. Living in New Mexico, I am even more removed from Aleppo: two thousand miles from my family in Maryland, and much further removed from the Syrian community in Brooklyn. My father's simple request launched myriad questions in my own mind about identity, family, and culture: what remains, what evolves, and what is left behind. This book reflects the outcome of my research, curiosity, and love.

Aleppo's Crowning Glory

s a child, my father did not know just how long his ancestors had been in Aleppo. Had they arrived with the wave of Jews fleeing the Spanish Inquisition in 1492? Had they predated those Spanish Jews, or come in recent generations for business opportunities? This wasn't a topic of conversation at home. He *did* know that the synagogue in Aleppo's Old City, large enough to accommodate hundreds of worshippers, had been functioning for over a thousand years—evidence of a sizeable Jewish community long before the influx of Jews from Spain.

Only when I started researching Aleppo did I learn of its glorious Jewish history, starting with stories in the Bible. Where had this history gone? I never heard a word of it in history classes, religious school, or family lore. The traumatic exodus of the Syrian Jews in the last century seemed to have collaborated with the Arab countries' virulent anti-Jewish drift to create amnesia about the country's Jewish history.

My urge to learn more about Syria's Jewish history stemmed first from my desire to learn more about my father and my people. But in doing so I discovered that in little more than the past half-century, Jewish communities that had existed in Syria for over two thousand years have emptied out. Between 1948 and the early 2000s, Syria's Jewish population went from thirty thousand to fewer than a hundred in the entire country. With no sustainable Jewish community in Syria, their history is too easily forgotten but simply too important to lose.

> **Between 1948 and the early 2000s, Syria's Jewish population went from thirty thousand to fewer than a hundred in the entire country.**

୧୬

A common legend in Jewish and Muslim tradition tells of Abraham passing through Aleppo on his journey to Canaan from his birthplace of Ur, and stopping to milk his cows on the side of a hill. Abraham, the tale says, went down that hill to distribute milk to the poor, leading to the most common account of the city's name: *Halib,* the Arabic word for milk, evolving into *Halab,* the city's Arabic name.

Another biblical legend, this one from the Book of Samuel, tells of King David conquering Aram Soba (the biblical name for Aleppo) and giving the city to his victorious general, Joab ben Seruyah, who built a synagogue there in 950 BCE. Today the Great Synagogue of Aleppo stands on that site on a foundation that legend says was laid by Joab himself. It still is referred to as Joab's Synagogue.

This is the huge synagogue that my father remembers as a young child living in Aleppo's Old City. The structure that now stands on the site was begun in the ninth century CE and expanded several times. For centuries it was the anchor of Aleppo's Jewish community, an architectural marvel with multiple assembly halls, windows overlooking fruit orchards and irrigation pools, and courtyards where services were held in good weather. The arrival of Jews from Spain required the construction of a new wing, where the newcomers prayed in their somewhat-different ways before assimilating into Aleppo's existing Jewish community. The Great Synagogue of Aleppo was one of the world's oldest continuously functioning synagogues until it was shuttered two decades ago when there were no longer enough Jews in the city to sustain a congregation.

୧୬

Aleppo's noted role in Jewish history is owed in large part to the fact that for nearly six hundred years, its Great Synagogue housed one of the major treasures of the Jewish tradi-

The Great Synagogue of Aleppo was one of the world's oldest continuously functioning synagogues until it was shuttered two decades ago when there were no longer enough Jews in the city to sustain a congregation.

tion. The Aleppo Codex, sometimes reverently referred to simply as the "Crown," from the Hebrew *Keter Aram Soba* for Crown of Aleppo, is considered the oldest surviving and most authoritative of the Biblical Jewish texts.

The codex form of manuscript was invented by the Romans in the first century, with handwritten leaves stitched together like a modern book to be much more portable and easier to navigate than tablets or scrolls. Over a thousand years ago, in the city of Tiberius in what is now Israel, a scribe copied the Torah and other Jewish texts into the manuscript that came to be the Aleppo Codex.

Since the Torah scrolls used in synagogues are handwritten with only the twenty-two letters of the Hebrew alphabet—but with no punctuation, vowels, or stress marks—the pronunciation of the words has always been passed down orally. The great contribution of the Aleppo Codex comes from its addition of punctuation, vowels, cantillation marks (written notation indicating the traditional intonation for chanting Hebrew prayers), and other margin notes explaining correct

Its courtyard shown here, the Great Synagogue of Aleppo stands on a foundation that legend says was laid by Joab ben Seruyah, a general of King David's, in 950 BCE. It still is referred to as Joab's Synagogue.

The Aleppo Codex. Shown here are pages 2 and 3 of the Book of Isaiah.

Hebrew pronunciation and inflection. This has provided an indispensible link in the continuity of Jewish practice, letting Jews pass down the Torah orally in a consistent way from generation to generation and country to country.

Crusaders stole the codex from Jerusalem in 1099 and took it to Egypt, where they held it for ransom (along with several prominent religious leaders and other Jewish holy works) until Egyptian Jews managed to buy it back. The great medieval Spanish scholar Moses Maimonides relied upon a book in Cairo when writing his *Mishneh Torah* (Re-

What's left of the codex currently resides at the Israel Museum in Jerusalem. When it resurfaced in 1958, almost 200 of its original 490 pages were missing.

view of the Torah) that he praised as "the well-known codex in Egypt that had been in Jerusalem for several years, and upon which all relied because it was proofread by [Aharon] Ben Asher, who worked on it carefully for many years and examined it again whenever it was being copied." Many assume that the codex Maimonides consulted is the one now known as the Crown of Aleppo.

In 1375, someone—perhaps one of Maimonides' descendants—transported the book from Cairo to Aleppo, by then already renowned as a center of Torah study. From then until

In March 1492, King Ferdinand and Queen Isabella issued the Alhambra Decree, which ordered Jews (and later Muslims) to leave Spain or convert to Catholicism.

the mid-1900s, the codex was kept in the Great Synagogue and treasured almost as a living being. People in crisis would stand before the codex to pray. Jews around the world would send questions about biblical passages they wanted checked against the manuscript that was considered the authoritative source. Eventually it was locked in an iron vault in an underground chapel that legend said was the cave of the prophet Elijah.

This is where it remained in safekeeping until riots erupted in Aleppo in late 1947, when the United Nations announced its decision to partition Palestine and create the State of Israel. The codex vanished. For months, people feared it had been destroyed. Although reports later emerged that at least part of it had been saved, its whereabouts were unknown for more than a decade, subject to rumor and speculation.

When it finally reappeared in 1958, in the hands of the Israel Museum in Jerusalem, almost two hundred of its original four hundred ninety pages were missing. Many questions remain: What happened to the codex? Where are its lost pages? Do they even still exist?

And theories abound as well. Some people claim that Israeli Jews stole it and took it to the new country, in the belief that its possession would strengthen their claim to the region. Others maintain that the missing pages disappeared only after it was transported to Israel and may have made their way to the black market. Still others cite an age-old prophecy that if the codex were ever removed from Aleppo, the city's Jewish community would be destroyed.

Questions remain, and pages are still missing. What *is* known is that most of the beloved codex is now in a place where it is secure, treasured, and available to scholars—and the Jews of Aleppo are no more.

❃

When King Ferdinand and Queen Isabella issued the Alhambra Decree in March 1492, ordering Jews (and later Muslims) to leave Spain or convert to Catholicism, many

Jews chose to remain, although more than a hundred fifty thousand fled. Some moved north to more-tolerant European regimes. Others went to the Americas, where in the hinterlands of the Spanish Empire, they outwardly professed Catholicism but continued Jewish practices for centuries. The greatest numbers fanned out across the Mediterranean into parts of the Ottoman Empire, which at the time spanned North Africa, Greece, Italy, Turkey, the Middle East, and the Balkan region.

Sultan Bajazet II, ruler of the Ottoman Empire, actually sent his navy to Spain in 1492 to transport Jews safely to Ottoman lands, and issued proclamations throughout the empire that the arriving Jews should be welcomed. He ridiculed the Spanish rulers for expelling a group of people that had been active in all levels of Spanish society, even high levels of government. "You venture to call Ferdinand a wise ruler," he scoffed to one of his advisers, "he who has impoverished his own country and enriched mine!"

Syria must have felt familiar to the Jews of the Spanish diaspora, since for nearly eight hundred years, Spain had been under Islamic control. The Umayyad Muslims who entered the Iberian Peninsula in the mid-eighth century, fleeing an uprising that had overthrown their leadership in Damascus, planted olive trees, pomegranates, and other crops they had brought with them from Syria along with advanced irrigation techniques, and constructed their homes and mosques in the style of their homeland. In the process they created what author Jane S. Gerber, in her book *Jews of Spain: A History of the Sephardic Experience,* calls "an extensive Syrianization of the entire Andalusian countryside." For centuries Arabic was in fact the *lingua franca* of scholarship and literature, government, science, mathematics, and commerce—the foundation for a thriving intellectual, literary, and artistic society in Spain while the rest of Europe was slogging through the Middle Ages.

The Jews arriving in Syria spoke a dialect of Castilian Spanish that has come to be known as Ladino—or, in the more-proper linguistic term, "Judeo-Spanish." Initially, they

Sultan Bajazet II, ruler of the Ottoman Empire, actually sent his navy to Spain in 1492 to transport Jews safely to Ottoman lands, and issued proclamations throughout the empire that the arriving Jews should be welcomed.

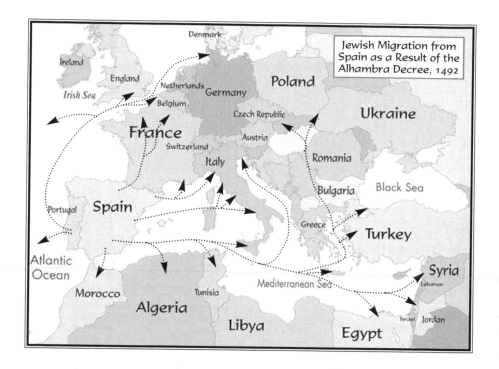

Jewish Migration from Spain as a Result of the Alhambra Decree, 1492

After the Alhambra Decree was issued in March 1492, more than a hundred fifty thousand Jews chose to leave Spain rather than convert to Catholicism. They spread out across the Old and New Worlds.

remained separate from the indigenous Jews in Aleppo, but gradually the communities converged. Linguistic scholars assume the Judeo-Spanish of the Spanish exiles in Aleppo blended into Arabic by the middle of the eighteenth century.

The Ottoman Turkish Empire took control of Syria in 1516 and ruled it for four hundred years. The Ottomans recognized Jews and Christians as fellow "People of the Book" and gave them the status of *dhimmi,* non-Muslims in an Islamic country who were allowed the right of residence in exchange for a special tax. Specific protocols of *dhimmi* status varied over time, but in general, the Jews were not granted the full rights of Muslims though they were largely autonomous and not required to serve in the military. They had their own court system, operated by local rabbis, and were officially allowed religious freedom. Their actual degree of freedom rose and fell according to the leaders of the day, but as a rule, Jews were free to participate in business, scholarship, and religion, and not restricted to locked ghettos as they were in much of Europe at this time.

ↂ

The first wave of Jewish emigration from Syria began in the late 1800s. An economic downturn had made it harder to make a living, while the movement to create a Jewish homeland in the Middle East increased anti-Semitism. In 1909, when the Ottomans for the first time required Jews to serve in the military, emigration accelerated. Single Jewish men typically left first, then sent for their family members once they had established a base in a new country. World War I halted emigration for a while, leaving some families separated until it ended.

Syria launched the Arab Revolt of 1916–18, with British aid and encouragement, bringing to an end four centuries of Ottoman rule. The Kingdom of Syria, created in March 1920 under Faisal bin Hussein (who later became the first king of Iraq), was the first modern country controlled by Arabs, with borders stretching from the Taurus Mountains in the north, in what is now Turkey, all the way south to the Sinai Desert. But it was just a flash of independence. In July of that year, French troops landed on Syria's Mediterranean coast, quickly defeating King Faisal and bringing the country under French control.

In 1916, France and Britain had crafted the Sykes-Picot Agreement proposing European spheres of influence in the Middle East.

What the Syrians did not know was that back in 1916, France and Britain had crafted the Sykes-Picot Agreement proposing European spheres of influence in the Middle East, if and when the Ottoman Empire collapsed. In April 1920, barely a month after declaration of the independent Syrian state, the major European powers hastily convened the San Remo Conference where they agreed to implement Sykes-Picot. The Arab Kingdom of Syria was divided into two. The northern half, encompassing contemporary Syria and Lebanon, was assigned to France. Palestine, in the southern half, was mandated to England, along with much of Jordan and Iraq.

Under the terms of the mandate, these countries were allowed nominal independence, while remaining dominated by the foreign power until they reached some to-be-determined level of maturity. In 1923, the League of Nations formalized this division, and Syria officially came under French control.

CB

The country into which my father was born (accounts vary as to whether it was in 1922 or 1924) was interlaced with Arab and European influences. France established the franc as the basis of the economy, issued French passports, and posted French flags around town. School children sang "La Marseillaise." Arabic remained the common language on the street, but French became the official language of the government and schools. At home with his mother, my father spoke Arabic. At school, he received lessons primarily in French. With his siblings and friends, he used both Arabic and French. His father used Arabic, French, and Turkish in his business. European fashions and cultural influences spread, while Arab nationalism continued to foment. I imagine the city at the time of my father's birth, just a few years after the end of the Ottoman Empire, in the early stages of French control, as a Syrian, French, and Turkish *tagine*.

> I imagine the city at the time of my father's birth, just a few years after the end of the Ottoman Empire, in the early stages of French control, as a Syrian, French, and Turkish *tagine*.

Sephardic? Mizrahi? What Are We?

rowing up, I always heard our family origins described as "Sephardic," the umbrella term for Jews of Middle Eastern origin. Most of the Jewish families living near us in Maryland—and the vast majority of Jews in the United States—were "Ashkenazi," that is, from Germany, Eastern Europe, and Russia. Common understanding held that all Middle Eastern Jews had relocated there from Spain after the Inquisition, and indeed, the term's root is *Sepharad*, the Hebrew word for Spain.

So when a teacher at my synagogue in Santa Fe offered a short course on the history of Spanish Jews, I signed up, expecting to fill in precious pieces in the puzzle of my own background. But several things I learned about Jews who had left after the Inquisition in 1492 did not mesh with what I knew of my family. The teacher told us that some communities of Spanish-Jewish exiles in Greece, Turkey, North Africa and the New World to this day still speak Ladino, the melodic Judeo-Spanish that evolved from the Castilian vernacular of pre-Inquisition Spain. He said the communities had maintained the language among themselves for centuries while also adopting the dominant tongue of their new country. Some five hundred years after expulsion, many descendants of Spanish Jews still refer to themselves as "Castellanos," meaning those whose families originated in Spain. Some, the teacher said, even keep keys to the ancestral family house in Spain, as a heart connection to the place they still consider home.

I signed up for a short course at my family's synagogue to learn about my own background. Several things I learned about Jews who had left after the Inquisition in 1492 did not mesh with what I knew of my family.

He described the Spain reflected in these Jews' passion as nearly tantamount to a second Holy Land. Yet I had never heard anyone in our family speak, or speak of, Ladino, and had never heard any of my relatives mention Spain or Spanish origins. Since I hadn't heard enough Arabic in our home to pick up more than a few words or phrases, I did not know what Spanish influences might have prevailed in their language.

When I asked my father what he had known of Ladino or Spanish roots back in Aleppo, he said he knew that some of their Arabic words had Spanish roots. (Their word *consuegra*, for mother-in-law, for instance, was almost the same as the Spanish word *suegra*). As for Ladino, he had never heard it in Aleppo, certainly not at home, and his parents never spoke of ancestry from Spain. In fact, he said, he had not heard the theory that Middle Eastern Jews originally came from Spain until he belonged to a predominantly Ashkenazi synagogue in Washington, D.C.

So if my family wasn't from Spain, I wondered—reluctant to relinquish ties to Cervantes, Goya, García Lorca, and Picasso—what were we?

The teacher in that synagogue class also introduced a term I had not heard before: Mizrahi. This classification of Jewish origins—distinct from Sephardic or Ashkenazi—categorized Jews indigenous to the Middle East, those whose ancestry there preceded the Spanish Inquisition, dating back in some cases to the Roman Empire. The word Mizrahi came into widespread use after the creation of Israel, he said, when large numbers of Jews began arriving from neighboring Arab countries with practices and traditions that differed widely from those followed by the Jews of Spanish descent, indicating very different ancestry.

Sephardic or Mizrahi? What are we? Without DNA tests or genealogical records going back hundreds of years, the question remains somewhat speculative. Spanish Jews *did* settle in Aleppo in great numbers, though they did not remain separated as in other Mediterranean and North African coun-

> **Sephardic or Mizrahi? What are we? Without DNA tests or genealogical records going back hundreds of years, the question remains somewhat speculative.**

tries—perhaps because Aleppo already had a large and relatively secure Jewish community. Within a couple of centuries, the Spanish Jews had comingled with Aleppo's
indigenous Jews, and bloodlines and languages were reshaped
by cultural crosscurrents and intermarriage.

My father, right,
with his Aunt
Ramiza and a
family friend,
circa 1940.

Perhaps in the end, the distinction between Sephardic
and Mizrahi has little significance, since the Jews of Spain
originally emigrated from the Middle East, to which many
of their descendants returned after the expulsion. To
Rabbi Marc D. Angel, founder of Sephardic House in
New York, a Sephardic Jew is "almost any Jew which is
not Ashkenazi"—implying that the underlying common-
alities of religious custom and belief are more significant
than any cultural or linguistic divergences that developed
over centuries in the countries where they lived since their
common ancestry.

From Spain or not, our family and others from Aleppo
can assume their roots have been there for at least five hundred years—and perhaps two thousand more. In any case,
because of this ambiguity about our ancestry, I do not refer

Jews from Aleppo can assume their roots have been there for at least five hundred years.

here to my family as Sephardic but as "Syrian Jewish"—a more cumbersome, perhaps less mellifluous but certainly more accurate, term.

A Place Within Generations

s a boy, my father wrote his name as shown above. From right to left, it reads: *Miro, son of Selim Sutton.* His given name was Meïr, a Hebrew name that he heard primarily in the synagogue, when the rabbis called him up to the Torah, and in the classroom, when called on by his teachers. Among friends and family, he went by Miro. Decades—and a world's journey—later, he would adopt the Western name he would go by for the rest of his life: Mike.

Miro, son of Selim Sutton—in the way so common in ancient cultures, a name that reflects not an individual identity but a child's place within generations of family. In keeping with the Syrian-Jewish tradition of naming the first-born son for his father's father, my dad was named for his paternal grandfather, Meïr Sittehon.

Each of his father's four brothers also had a son named Meïr. (The family name written in Arabic was pronounced like "Sittehon" in Hebrew, "Sitton" in Arabic, "Soutton" in French, and "Sutton" in English.) My father was called Miro as a young child, a common nickname for Meïr. And so his

> Miro, son of Selim Sutton— in the way so common in ancient cultures, a name that reflects not an individual identity but a child's place within generations of family.

everyday signature, *Miro, son of Selim Sutton,* reflected not just his familial nickname but also a way of honoring his father and grandfather.

Selim's wife, Adele (née Laniado), gave birth to her first child, my father, in either 1922 or 1924. At the time, the Syrian government did not issue birth certificates, though Jewish boys might have an approximate birth date recorded at the synagogue when they were circumcised, while a daughter's birth might not be recorded at all. Families rarely kept precise birth records, and the date of his birth has become unclear. He always seemed to consider his year of birth as being 1922, although his passport says 1924. When his siblings came to America years later, they simply made up birthdates for their passport applications.

After my dad, two sons followed, Saleh and Elie; a daughter, Margo; then four more sons, Ralph, Joe, Morris, and Edgar. Such large families were typical in the community, though seven boys and one girl was not! My grandmother Adele became a mother at fifteen and continued bearing children for more than two decades. My father never met his youngest sibling, Edgar, who was born after Dad left Syria for Shanghai and who died in Lebanon as a young teen.

What did Aleppo feel, smell and sound like in the early decades of the twentieth century? Joseph A.D. Sutton (no relation to our family) gives us a sense in *Aleppo Chronicles:*

"Aleppo is set on the high plain, with low humidity. Thus, walking with an uncovered head under the summer sun is known to cause sunstroke; while, sitting in the shade of a tree (or under the roofed *souks*) is a delightful, cool experience. Picnicking in the *basateen,* the orchards, at the outskirts of Aleppo, is available to all with the payment of a very small fee, which includes apricots, figs, and other fruits in abundance as well. Mulberries (*toot,* cultivated for the ancient silk manufacture), pistachio nuts, walnuts (so very sweet and tender when plucked off the trees), all available free to the picnickers. Springtime and autumn were the best seasons. On a rare cloudy day in the summer,

My dad was born in either 1922 or 1924. At the time, the Syrian government did not issue birth certificates, though Jewish boys might have an approximate birth date recorded at the synagogue when they were circumcised, while a girl's birth might not be recorded at all.

Aleppo residents would exclaim, 'What a beautiful day for a *bistan* [garden] party!'"

Muslim observances also lit up the streets: "Frequent Muslim religious celebrations would see the city festooned with lights; streets were crowded with the celebrants commemorating some Islamic saint. Like street festivals everywhere, there were foodstuffs to be bought, and entertainment, jugglers and acrobats performing." Sutton emphasizes that peaceful relations between Jews and Muslims ruled Aleppo in the early part of the century, particularly among the educated and those who had contact through business dealings or private schools.

White stone houses, marvels of Ottoman architecture and natural sun-proofing, lined the twisty streets in the city's oldest neighborhoods. As author Lynn Simarski describes it, "Impassive stone walls like dikes channel the flow of traffic and conceal the quiet charm of the homes behind them— Aleppo's finest collection of Arab houses from the seventeenth and eighteenth centuries. Heavy, half-open doors reveal elegant courtyards and fountains. . . . The limestone houses, generally of one or two stories, nestle back-to-back

Family portrait, circa 1946. Top row from left, Joe, Ralph, Margo. Bottom row, Morris, Grandmother Adele, Grandfather Selim, and Edgar

"But when you
talk about
someplace like
Aleppo," Dad
said, "it was
a small town
where
everybody
knew most
everybody, or
knew of them."

to minimize the expanse of wall exposed to sun. Privacy is paramount, so many entrance passageways twist to block courtyards from direct public view. Inside, patios are paved with contrasting flagstones. Citrus trees, jasmine, and roses grow in basins near fountains or pools. In wealthy homes, a musicians' stand in the courtyard was used for concerts."

My father remembers the tranquil flow of daily life in the Aleppo of his youth. Men walked to work; children walked or rode bikes to school. The first home he remembers was an apartment in Aleppo's Old City, set around a shared interior courtyard, similar to a Spanish hacienda. This was a typical housing arrangement in the oldest parts of town, where each family had its own quarters around a common open area, sharing a kitchen and outhouse. In some cases, the neighbors might be related, but more often, they were not.

"But when you talk about someplace like Aleppo," Dad said, "it was a small town where everybody knew most every-

body, or knew *of* them. In a setup such as this, they would become friends and get along well." Everyone in the Jewish community shared religious traditions and an acceptance of the family as the central pillar.

"This apartment was our home for some two or three years," he said. "Though quite comfortable, the location was not ideal for growing tots. At the time, Saleh and I were the only siblings. It overlooked a busy section of downtown Aleppo. We overlooked the street where horse-drawn carriages were parked, to be hired for transportation. It was noisy during the day and into late evenings."

Families typically lived with or near their grandparents, cousins, and other relatives. Not surprisingly, my father's earliest memories are of large gatherings for holidays and Sabbath celebrations.

"I remember one instance during a Friday night dinner when I asked my father what he was drinking, and he gave me some to try," Dad said. "It was arak. Arak is a Near East-

Situated on a high, arid plain, Aleppo has been inhabited for 5,000 years, excavations show.

ern drink that tastes like anise. It's heavily alcoholic, and it's potent." (Here I must ask if family history really does repeat itself. I reminded my dad of a big party at our house when I was about eight at which I asked what the drink in his glass was. "Ginger ale," he answered sweetly, leaning down to offer me a sip. I felt I had swallowed fire. It was gin. "I guess I had to get even with somebody," Dad said with a coy smile.)

The city's Jewish, Muslim, and Christian communities lived by choice in separate districts. There were no walled ghettos, no gates enclosing or separating neighborhoods, but everyone knew which belonged to whom, and residents generally kept to their own. Men of different religions dealt with one another in business, and their children might go to school together, but close friendships generally stayed within, not between, the groups. There seemed to be a tacit agreement for benevolent separation.

CB

My grand-father, Selim Sutton, was an importer of textiles from Europe and neighboring countries. "Piece-goods," Dad explained, "in other words, fabrics that came by the rolls."

My grandfather, Selim Sutton, was an importer of textiles from Europe and neighboring countries. "Piece-goods," Dad explained, "in other words, fabrics that came by the rolls." He traveled frequently for his business when Dad was young, primarily to Turkey and Europe. The textile trade—particularly silk, wool, and cotton—had been integral to Syrian commerce for centuries, since Aleppo's days on the Silk Road. Wholesale fabrics were essential to everyday life since people rarely bought ready-made clothing off the rack. They would buy material to sew into clothes for themselves and their families or arrange to have garments custom-made by local tailors.

In 1927, my grandfather moved the family to Mersin, Turkey, a port on the Mediterranean Sea not far across the border from Syria, and set up his business there. My father was five years old, as he tells it, his brother Saleh was about three, and his brother Elie was still a baby. Their sister, Margo, was born in Turkey. ("Funny how some things you

never forget," Dad said of his sister's birth. "There was a mid-wife in the room. I said it was a girl, and they shushed me!")

"In Mersin, the family lived in a spacious apartment with a garden, not far from my father's office," Dad said. "I was still too young to go to school, so Saleh and I played around the house. Not far from Dad's office was the seashore, where I enjoyed spending some time walking the beach.

"About a year or so later, I started school, but Saleh was still too young to go. The teacher was a nice-looking blonde, and I think I had a crush on her. She scolded me for doing something I wasn't supposed to do, and I was crushed. Of course, I forgot what it was."

Although the move did not take them geographically far from Aleppo, it was a great distance culturally. The little city had only a small Jewish community, and the people there, although mostly Muslim, were not Arabs and spoke Turkish rather than Arabic. Starting school in Mersin as a young boy, my father took classes taught entirely in Turkish. His brother Saleh was also soon speaking Turkish. "At one point," Dad

Aleppo's modern-day Al-Madina Souk market. The textile trade—particularly silk, wool, and cotton—has been integral to Syrian commerce for centuries, since Aleppo's days on the Silk Road.

Although it was only five hours from Aleppo, Mersin was a great distance culturally. Major roads (solid gray) and train routes (dashed gray) are shown here.

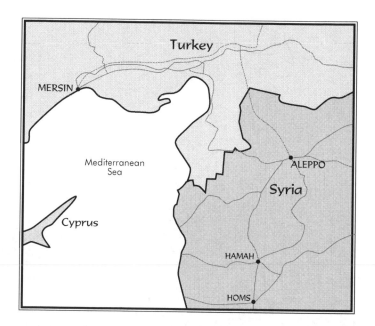

remembered, "my mother said, 'You kids better speak some Arabic, because if you don't, you're going to forget it, speaking Turkish all the time!'"—perhaps a mom's overstatement, since the family spoke Arabic in the home.

Turkey was just a fledgling country at the time, established in 1923, after the collapse of the Ottoman Empire, as a secular, democratic republic—unique among its neighbors. My father remembered the changes under its first president, Mustafa Kemal Atatürk, whose goal was to modernize and Westernize the country.

"He made it a law for women not to wear veils on their faces like they do in other Muslim countries," Dad said. "Men could wear hats, but they had to be European-style hats, not the fez, which was the predominant headgear in those days."

Before Atatürk, the Turkish language was written with Arabic characters, but he substituted the Western alphabet, with modifications for phonetic spelling that made it very easy to learn. As a result, literacy rates soared.

"Take for example," Dad said, "the simple English word, 'through.' The way that you pronounce it is not at all the way you spell it. But in the modernized Turkish alphabet, there were no two letters to form one sound. 'S' by itself was pronounced 's,' but an 's' with a jigger under it was 'sh.' 'C' by itself was a 'c,' but with a jigger under it, it was 'ch.' And so on. It simplified learning to spell and to read and write."

Though he learned some of these things later, even as a child, he knew Atatürk was an extremely popular leader. "Let me tell you about something that happened when I was a school kid," Dad said. "We were told to dress in our school uniform to meet the president of Turkey, who was coming by boat to the port of Mersin, where we lived." Children from all the schools in town wore the same uniform, he explained, with a hat similar to a pilot's cap, but each school identified itself by a band around the cap with its name on it. "We were to go out on a pier and welcome the president. It was exciting to see him—picture today you're a kid and the president of the United States comes to visit. The schoolchildren went out on a pier to wave to the president when his ship arrived in the port."

My father and his classmates waited on the pier to see the president—and waited and waited. When Atatürk finally arrived, the children could only see him and wave from a distance. Still, the excitement of the anticipation stayed with him.

"Life in Turkey was good," Dad recalled, "and my father was doing well. The only drawback was that we did not have any Hebrew education. Mersin had a small synagogue, which we went to on Saturdays and holidays, but with such a small community, there obviously was not much opportunity for Jewish education."

So when he was about eight years old, his parents sent him and Saleh back to Aleppo to live with their maternal grandmother and attend Hebrew school.

"Going to Grandma was not exactly hard," Dad said. "It was more like a picnic, being spoiled by a grandmother and so forth. But after a while, you start to miss your mother and father, and you wish to be with them again."

> "Life in Turkey was good," Dad recalled, "and my father was doing well. The only drawback was that we did not have any Hebrew education."

When Dad, at
right with a
cousin, was
about eight
years old, his
parents sent him
and Saleh back
to Aleppo to live
with their
maternal
grandmother
and attend
Hebrew school.

Apparently, their mother missed them, too. Within a month, Adele went back to Aleppo by train to pick up the two boys and take them home to Mersin. Soon afterward, the whole family returned to Aleppo so the children could be raised with a Jewish education.

The Head of the Fish

eturning to school in Aleppo, my father and his brother Saleh entered a private Jewish elementary school affiliated with the synagogue near their home, an all-boy's school that went through the eighth grade. Despite their two-year age difference, both were placed in the same grade because they had never attended classes taught in Arabic before. After four years in Turkey, where classes had been taught entirely in Turkish, Dad and Saleh had to learn Hebrew and French on the quick. Classes were conducted in French and Arabic, and at the end of the school day, all the students gathered in the hallway and recited Hebrew prayers before school was adjourned.

The family lived in several apartments over the next few years before settling at a house in the Jamiliyeh district on what was then the outskirts of Aleppo. Jewish families had begun moving earlier in the century from the hacienda-style homes in the Old City to Jamiliyeh, which had more open space.

"This section of Aleppo was quite different from the one we knew before we left for Turkey," Dad recalled. "It was the newer section, with much wider streets and newer, more comfortable living space and surroundings. Streetcars were the mode of transportation, and later automobiles. Horse-drawn carriages were no longer the main mode of transportation but more for leisure rides through town during nice weather."

The family lived in a large, stone house on a main thoroughfare where Jewish and Arab neighborhoods met. A Muslim family lived next door, and a mosque stood across the

When they returned to Aleppo, the family lived in a large, stone house on a main thoroughfare where Jewish and Arab neighborhoods met. A Muslim family lived next door, and a mosque stood across the street.

street. The streetcar passed in front of the house, stopping
practically at their door. My grandfather's two older brothers,
Hillel and Abraham, had built the house but transferred it
to my grandfather to repay a large sum of money he'd loaned
them to start a textile business. (The business had gone under
and they moved to Palestine with their families and mother.)

Approaching the house, a visitor would go up a few steps
to a small porch outside the front door, where my father's
maternal grandmother often sat sipping coffee or smoking
tobacco through a *nargilleh*, a Turkish water pipe. From the
porch, one might watch the streetcar or horse-drawn carriages or people on foot or bike. Few people had their own
cars, but occasional taxis passed by taking people around the
city or on short excursions out of town.

A central hallway with marble floors divided the house's
six large rooms: the master bedroom, another bedroom and
the living room to the right; two more bedrooms and a dining room to the left. As the family grew and the kids got
older, they shifted among the bedrooms. Double doors at
the end of the hallway opened onto an outdoor patio where
the family ate meals in the warmer months. In Aleppo's
semi-desert climate, summers are hot and dry, and winters
are cool and wet but rarely drop below freezing, ideal for
an outdoor patio. The house had a full basement with the
same layout, originally built for living space but used instead only for storage. To the left of the front entrance,
there was a staircase leading up to the roof. The house was
built to accommodate a second floor that could be rented
out as a separate unit, but in the meantime the family used
the roof as another outdoor patio in warm months.

Theirs was the first house in the neighborhood to have indoor plumbing, which they added soon after moving in. Before that, they drew water from a well on the patio, and
continued to use it for refrigeration. "We had a bucket on a
rope," Dad said. "We would put things in there and get them
half-submerged below the surface, but you had to be careful
the water didn't get into the bucket." The only other way to

> **Their house
> was the first
> one in the
> neighborhood
> to have indoor
> plumbing,
> which they
> added soon
> after moving
> in. Before that,
> they drew
> water from a
> well on the
> patio, which
> they continued
> to use for
> refrigeration.**

keep food cool was an icebox in the kitchen, stocked with blocks from the iceman. My father and the other neighborhood boys played soccer and flew kites on a big field next door.

The family often gathered on the rooftop patio of their Aleppo home. From left are Morris, Edgar, their mother Adele, father Selim, Joe, and Ralph, circa 1946.

℘

Life in Aleppo's close-knit Jewish community was easygoing and relaxed. "Men did not seem to work hard," Dad recalled. "They were able to come home for lunch, return home early again for dinner, and socialize a lot. Religious holidays were celebrated with joy, times to see friends and relatives and receive visitors." Boys walked to the synagogue, just three blocks from their house, and then school, barely a dozen blocks away. There was a synagogue in walking distance of every Jewish home since Orthodox families would not drive or ride public transportation on the Sabbath. When a neighborhood grew to the point that residents could not walk to the synagogue, someone would commission a new Torah for religious services in his home and hire a rabbi to lead them until a new synagogue could be built.

"To be religious was the norm," Dad explained. "Fridays

Grandmother
Adele and Saleh
on the front
steps of the
Aleppo house,
circa 1946.

were usually spent getting ready for the Sabbath. Women spent the day in the kitchen cooking some five or six different dishes for the Friday night dinner, while also preparing the Saturday feast, which was eaten after coming out of *shul* around noon." A typical Friday night meal might include chicken; rice and *hamud;* fish; vegetables such as beans, peas, okra, or eggplant; and stuffed eggplant, squash, or grape leaves. For Saturday's lunch, after the men and boys had returned from the synagogue, his mother would serve some of Friday's leftovers, another main dish—perhaps pot roast or chicken—and two or three other side dishes.

The Friday night meal began after sundown when the men came home from the synagogue. After saying blessings for the food and wine, and the long prayer welcoming the Sabbath, the family would wish one another Good Sabbath—first youngsters to elders, then vice versa. Children would kiss the hands of adults and greet one another respectfully.

With services at the synagogue, more prayers at home, and a feast of so many dishes, Friday dinner lasted late into the night. When everyone was ready for bed, someone would step out the front door to look for someone walking by whom they could ask to come in and turn off the main switch for the house's electricity. Everybody in town knew that the Jews did not turn lights on or off or work on the Sabbath, so a passerby—most likely a non-Jew, since Jews would be home with their own families—would understand the request. The passerby would turn off the switch-box by the front door, which would stay off until someone in the family turned it back on after sundown Saturday evening when the Sabbath was over.

"At the conclusion of the Saturday morning services, I would walk with one or two of my brothers to my grandma's house for a short visit before returning home for lunch," Dad said. "I should explain that when I make reference to 'Grandma' I am referring to my mother's mother. Father's mother was living in Palestine, where she moved soon after our return from Turkey." Out of custom, they would pay their grandmother a visit, kiss her hands, and wish her "Good Sabbath." Then they would go home for the big afternoon meal, which their mother would have kept on a slow-burning fire since sundown the previous day until her husband and sons returned from Saturday services.

After the Sabbath lunch, young people would gather to socialize on a particular street not far from the family's house. On Saturday nights after the Sabbath had ended, and on Sundays and holidays, men met at one of two nearby cafes to play cards or *toleh* (backgammon) and socialize. Women visited in their homes, perhaps playing cards or sitting on the porch smoking a pipe.

Everybody in town knew that the Jews did not turn lights on or off or work on the Sabbath, so a passerby — most likely a non-Jew, since Jews would be home with their own families — would turn off the switch-box by the front door.

The life of
Aleppo's Jews
was peppered
with prayer from
sunup to sun-
down. They
would say
prayers at
morning light;
often at the Great
Synagogue
(shown here)
before school;
in the afternoon,
which my father's
elementary
schoolmates
recited together
in the hallway at
the end of the
day; and just
after sunset.

Religious observance and celebration infused the whole town, Dad recalled. Muslims observed the month of Ramadan every year, when they would fast from sunrise to sunset. Since the Islamic calendar is a strictly lunar one, without a "leap month" to match up to the solar cycles as the Jewish calendar has, Ramadan can fall at any point during the year. When it landed during the school year, as it usually did, Dad's Muslim classmates would get up before sunrise to pray and have breakfast, then fast until after sundown. The Islamic call to prayer would be heard all over Aleppo, five times every day: just before sunrise, at noon, in the late afternoon, at sunset, and before bed. Each time, Muslims would stop what they were doing and pray, whether at the mosque or at their school, home, or business.

The life of the city's Jews was likewise peppered with prayer from sunup to sundown. They would say prayers at morning light; often at synagogue before school; in the afternoon, which my father's elementary schoolmates recited together in the hallway at the end of the day; and just after sunset. They would wash their hands before every meal, recite the prayer over the bread, and pray after eating. Sabbath and holidays brought additional sets of prayers. For the month before Rosh Hashanah, men and boys went to services well before dawn to recite *selichot*—prayers to prepare for the Yom Kippur fast and ask forgiveness for sins of the previous year.

Few in the Jewish community chose not to observe these practices, Dad said, though the exceptions did not necessarily generate the harsh judgment I might have expected. For instance, he remembers being sent by his father on an errand one Saturday after synagogue, to a government office with a boy who lived next door whose father needed a permit for work on his house. Since the Muslim day of rest is Friday, Saturday is a regular workday, and for reasons now forgotten, the permit needed to be obtained that day, perhaps because their fathers didn't want the boys to have to miss school. Dad would not have considered riding the streetcar on the Sabbath, so he walked more than an hour to the government building, though the neighbor, who was also Jewish, took the streetcar.

On the other hand, one year on the High Holy Days, the director of the Jewish high school, who had just arrived from France, drove to the synagogue on Rosh Hashanah morning, generating such sharp criticism that he never did it again.

Another man in the community, who lived just half a block from the synagogue, did not observe Jewish customs or go to services until well into his sixties. A neighbor, surprised to see him there after so many years, asked why. "I do not believe in all this," he answered with a dismissive wave of his hand, "but I have to make my peace with God before I die."

Although school was not compulsory in Syria (even in the primary grades), within the Jewish community, education was of the utmost importance — at least for boys.

ભ

Although school was not compulsory in Syria (even in the primary grades), within the Jewish community, education was of the utmost importance—at least for boys. Dad's sister, Margo, attended a girls' elementary school while her brothers went to the boys' school at their synagogue. Dad remembers a few Jewish girls in his high school, but by college, the few young women in his classes were Christian—not surprising given that Jewish women often married and started families as young as their early teens.

After completing the Jewish elementary school, many of my father's classmates enrolled in the Alliance Française, a Jewish secondary school. My father and Saleh tested into the more-challenging Mission Laïque Française/Lycée d'Alep— the Aleppo High School of the French Secular Mission. (The Mission Laïque, a worldwide network of secular schools established in 1902 to integrate French language and culture with studies in the language of the home country, still exists in many cities around the world.)

Dad and his brother placed into a grade above that of their friends at the Alliance Française. "This, of course, had its disadvantages," he recalled. "In order for us to keep up in higher grades, my father engaged a private tutor. It all paid off well because by the end of the year, I was first in class, and my brother, Saleh, was second. That carried through to the next grades, and school was more fun as a consequence."

Students at the Mission Laïque included Jews, Muslims, and Christians of Greek Orthodox, Catholic, and Armenian background, in a very modern building with large classrooms. The school did not require a uniform, but students dressed formally: boys in jackets and sweaters, girls in good dresses. Classes from 8 a.m. to noon were conducted in French. Students then bicycled home for lunch and returned for classes taught in Arabic until 5 p.m. Two evenings a week, my father and Saleh met privately with a rabbi to learn Hebrew. Though a nondenominational school, the Mission Laïque made accommodations for religious observance. School was in session for half a day on Saturday, but it was understood that the Jewish students would not be there. "As a result, little of consequence was taught that day," Dad said, "and classes were devoted mostly to review."

Outside of school, children of different religious backgrounds rarely mingled. Schools did not organize afterschool activities or sports teams that might have encouraged cross-cultural friendships, as American schools do today. When the school day ended, everyone went home.

"It would have been more educational to have a mixture

Classes from 8 a.m. to noon were conducted in French. Students then bicycled home for lunch and returned for classes taught in Arabic until 5 p.m.

of religions as friends," Dad said, "but that could not happen in the Middle East. The separation, though not planned, of the parts of Aleppo into quarters of Jews, Muslims, and Christians, made it impractical to have friends of another religion. As a result, we never really ventured into the areas where the Arabs or the Christians lived, and very few of them came into the Jewish quarter. Those who did come were just being mischievous, trying to pick a fight, so we tried to stay away from them. Mixed relationships or intermarriage would not have been tolerated by either camp."

Men's work provided more opportunity to know members of other religions, but there, too, those relations only went so far.

"Business was business," Dad said. When his father came home from his office, the family would sit down to dinner together, and then his father would often go to a cafe to meet friends and play backgammon, "but I think for the most part, that would be Jewish people." However, a Muslim family lived just behind my dad's house, and a window overlooked their backyard. "They were able to get a permit to build a wall alongside our back wall, to block the view of their yard from our house. I assume this was for privacy, because they didn't want us to look at their women."

What Dad did *not* see growing up was animosity between the Muslim groups fighting so viciously in Syria today. "We didn't know there was a difference between a Sunni and a Shiite," he said. "To us, a Muslim was a Muslim. We didn't get any sense that they hated each other."

What Dad did *not* see growing up was animosity between the Muslim groups fighting so viciously in Syria today. "We didn't know there was a difference between a Sunni and a Shiite."

CB

When my son reached adolescence and began going out with friends on weekends, I mentioned to my father that his grandsons had freedoms—later curfews, more sleepovers and parties—that my siblings and I did not have at their age.

"This is the pattern of the generations," Dad responded with his customary light-handedness. As teens, he and his friends would get together at a social hall or each other's houses for dance parties. Young people were starting to be able to choose their own spouses—liberties unknown to his mother and father. They had been betrothed in marriage by their parents, had no say in the union, and, in fact, did not even meet before the engagement was announced. So, as circumscribed as my father's social life might seem to his grandchildren, his generation had liberties that at times must have alarmed their parents.

"Teen-agers met on the street, walking with friends and socializing with acquaintances," Dad said. "Periodically, a friend would have a party where we would dance to records played on a Victrola. We anteed up some cash and periodically bought records for dancing. You never dated one-on-one unless you were engaged to be married."

Men typically married after establishing themselves in business and accumulating some money, but for women, the transition from childhood to adulthood happened practically overnight.

"Sometimes a young man who was either adventuresome or had an uncle or older relative abroad would travel and return a few years later having made his fortune, ready to get married," Dad recalled. "He would pick a much younger girl and marry her. I remember when I was about fourteen or fifteen years old, I knew a friend's sister who was no older than fourteen and looked even younger, with never a touch of lipstick or makeup. She was what we might call a tomboy today. She was one of us. We used to play marbles and other games together. Then one day, some young man returned from abroad, and the next thing we knew, she was engaged to him. When we saw her all made up, we didn't recognize her. She looked a lot older but awkwardly so." Their families had arranged the marriage, probably with the help of a hired matchmaker.

By the time Dad reached his teens, the tradition of arranged marriages was beginning to crumble, but parents still watched their children's social lives closely. The selection of a spouse still depended largely on economic status. He re-

> "Periodically, a friend would have a party where we would dance to records played on a Victrola. We anteed up some cash and periodically bought records for dancing."

members his mother and father as more liberal than most, but like all parents of their day, they weighed their children's options carefully. His mother did not let him attend the party of a girl he knew only casually because she felt the girl's family would not be of adequate standing for him to marry, should it come to that. He remembers the great discomfort of having to decline the invitation, although all his friends were allowed to go. If he had stayed in Syria, he assumes he would have been free to choose his own wife, since things were moving in that direction—provided both sets of parents gave their consent.

"We did not think to rebel," Dad said. "There was no such thing. A parent's word was absolute." A child's urge to protest would surely have been tempered by awareness that none of his or her peers questioned parental decisions either. Children were not asked whether they wanted to go to religious school or what school they would attend; these choices were made by parents and announced as the final word. No one would accuse Syrian parents of the day of coddling their children, though their love was undeniable. Dad describes his father as stern, showing his disapproval "never by striking or yelling but by his expression. If he stared at you in a certain way, you knew you had done something wrong." Yet overall, he remembers him as a compassionate man and a gentleman, who established a strong relationship with his sons as an advisor in schooling, learning and religious practice. He was less directly involved in his daughter's upbringing, since girls and women had no special prayers in religious observances or other roles for the Sabbath and holidays other than preparing meals, but Dad remembers him being as attentive to her as to the boys, taking her to numerous doctors in search of treatment for elephantiasis in her foot, a disease that caused her to walk with a pronounced limp.

"I loved him a lot," Dad said, quickly acknowledging that those words were not said in the home as they are today. "It was taken for granted that you were loved, and you loved in return."

> Dad describes his father as stern, showing his disapproval "never by striking or yelling but by his expression. If he stared at you in a certain way, you knew you had done something wrong."

My grandmother had her babies at home, like all women of the time. This photo was taken by my dad at about age 12, probably of his baby brother Joe, circa 1935.

His mother was more demanding and critical—particularly of her eldest son. "If the head of the fish doesn't smell good, the whole fish is rotten," she often told him, emphasizing the responsibility of setting an example for his siblings and representing the family well in the community. "I felt that Mother was a little strict with me but not as strict with Saleh," Dad said, "while the opposite was true where Dad was concerned."

In general, being the oldest seems to have brought my dad more sense of burden than pride. Other people thought of him as a well-behaved boy, though he remembers his good manners as stemming from shyness and pressure to uphold his parents' high expectations. His younger brothers had less of a spotlight on them, he said, and as a result, they were more playful, less reserved. "It's nice to be well-behaved," Dad said, glancing off reflectively, "but it's more fun to be impish."

⌘

The neighborhood synagogue served as an anchor in the family's lives. It accommodated over three hundred people, all living close enough so they would not have to drive or ride on the Sabbath. Every day, my father and his brothers woke early and said morning prayers at home or at the synagogue before going to school. In the evening, boys would go to synagogue before dinner. On Monday and Thursday mornings, men read a passage from the Torah at the synagogue.

"Hebrew education was so matter-of-fact that nothing was voluntary or optional about it," Dad said. "You automatically enrolled and studied Hebrew, and you went to synagogue every day—or most every day, not just holidays or special occasions. Sabbath was observed without reservations. The degree of being religious varied from person to person but not appreciably. So when a boy became of bar mitzvah age, he attended services on that day with relatives as well as members of the family. During the services, the bar mitzvah boy would be called to the Torah with special chanting. After the conclusion of services, refreshments were served to everyone. The family then had a special meal."

Boys could have a bar mitzvah ceremony any time after they entered their thirteenth year. Since they had been reciting prayers regularly at home and in the synagogue from when they were young, the service was hardly their initiation into Jewish practice. Instead, it marked the young man's acceptance as an adult member of the community, able to serve in a *minyan*, the quorum of ten or more men needed for certain religious observances. It also began the boy's ritual of reciting weekday morning prayers wearing *tefillin* (phylacteries, in English)—small leather boxes containing scripture

"Hebrew education was so matter-of-fact that nothing was voluntary or optional about it," Dad said. "You automatically enrolled and studied Hebrew, and you went to synagogue every day."

passages which are wrapped around the forehead and arm with leather straps. Bar mitzvah ceremonies would always take place on a Monday or Thursday. (Bat mitzvah ceremonies for girls did not exist.) The boy would stand alongside as the rabbi read the daily Torah portion but did not read from the Torah himself.

My father and his cousin Hillel, the son of his father's brother Abraham, had their bar mitzvah ceremonies together when Dad was twelve and Hillel was thirteen. The men in the families stayed home from work that day, and everyone walked together to the synagogue where they sang special songs and recited prayers. The boys were called up to the pulpit one at a time to stand beside the rabbi as he read the Torah portion. He then gave each boy a bag of candies, symbolizing the sweetness of the Torah. After sharing cake with their families and others at the synagogue, the families gathered in one of the boys' homes for a celebratory lunch.

Girls and women were not expected to attend the services. Some women went for the morning Torah readings, or on Friday night or Saturday morning, and others went only on holidays. By Orthodox practice, women and men sat separately in the synagogue. Women did not say the prayers or learn to read Hebrew. At the services, they would listen, talk with one another, and perhaps observe in a private, quiet way.

My father and his cousin Hillel, the son of his father's brother Abraham, had their bar mitzvah ceremonies together when Dad was twelve and Hillel was thirteen.

ℭ

From his earliest memories until he left home, my father has no recollection of his mother without babies and young children.

My grandmother had her babies at home, like all women of the time. Families treated illnesses or ailments themselves, calling a doctor only if someone was very ill and did not respond to the range of home remedies. My dad remembers people mobbing a doctor's car and besieging him with questions when he was called to see his great-grandmother, who was very sick. "You would not stop him for yourself but for a sick relative," Dad explained, "and they would probably be *really* sick if you were going to stop the doctor."

The family had a housekeeper who helped with cleaning and cooking, a Jewish woman who lived in the house and even moved with them when they went to Turkey. With few conveniences or appliances, however, household work consumed most of the day. Women would boil dirty linens in a big pot and hang them outside to dry. On Friday, they washed the house's marble floors to prepare for the Sabbath. With only the icebox and well to keep food cool, cooking strict kosher meals for such a large family and preparing for the large number of holidays consumed much of the day.

Women cooked hot dishes at home in a charcoal-heated oven, but bread was baked in a large communal oven near the house on Tuesdays and Friday mornings. My grandmother or the housekeeper would put a large batch of dough in a bin to rise in the evening, then the next morning would pat it into round, flat loaves of "pita bread"—now ubiquitous in American groceries but simply "Syrian bread" when we were children. One of the boys would carry a bin with the prepared loaves to the communal oven and bring back the fresh-baked bread later in the day. On Fridays, when cheese was in season because the goats were breeding and lactating, they would slide slices of fresh goat cheese inside a dozen or so of the unbaked loaves and take them to the oven for a delicious hot grilled sandwich before school.

Early each morning in calving season, a farmer would pass down the street with his cow on the way to market. Neighbors would come out with bottles to fill with fresh milk. Sometimes women made yogurt or *labneh* (yogurt thickened by straining out some of the liquid) from the fresh milk. In early spring when goats were milking, farmers would pass by the house selling slices from large blocks of goat cheese made just that morning or the day before. The family might buy a chunk of cheese to heat at home to soften and then pull apart into long, thin strands of "string cheese."

Typically, they ate lamb, not beef or goat. For meat to be

Women cooked hot dishes at home in a charcoal-heated oven, but bread was baked in a large communal oven near the house on Tuesdays and Friday mornings.

"koshered," it must be washed and salted before cooking, even if it was bought from a kosher butcher. Broiling or grilling meat was considered a way to make it kosher, allowing Jews to eat meat grilled on skewers by street vendors regardless of the meat's origins.

In earlier times, most shopping was done at the *souk*, the city's ancient marketplace with miles of covered walkways, but as people began moving farther out from the Old City, new shopping districts opened up to accommodate them. Men typically did the shopping. Since the grocers and other merchants were all men, Dad explained, and business was conducted by bargaining, everyone assumed that men would be more forceful bargainers. When their father was away on business, one of the boys or another man in the family would go to small shops near the house for their mother to pick up produce, cheeses, yogurt, and traditional Middle Eastern sweets like Turkish Delight and halvah.

Pre-made clothes were not available to families when Dad was young. By the time he reached his teens, store-bought clothes had become more common. Before that, most men had suits and shirts made to order by a local tailor, and women sewed clothes for their children and themselves. The local cobbler would measure their feet, present a selection of styles and colors, and then have the finished pair of shoes ready to pick up several days later—although this tradition, too, was in transition during my father's childhood. An outlet of Bata, one of the world's largest shoe companies, was just opening up in Aleppo when Dad was a teen.

One night on a recent visit to my parents, I watched them both floss their teeth at the same time before going to bed. Dad recalled that all through his childhood, he never brushed his teeth. No one did. Only when he lived in Shanghai and visited a dentist because of gum pain did he learn how to use a toothbrush, and why. He promptly wrote home instructing his parents and siblings on the importance of dental hygiene—perhaps his most poignant illustration of Aleppo's balance in the early twentieth century between the modern and the archaic.

> **Men typically did the shopping. Since the grocers and other merchants were all men, Dad explained, and business was conducted by bargaining, everyone assumed that men would be more forceful bargainers.**

Leaving Aleppo

mong a people characterized by the image of the "Wandering Jew," the Jews of Aleppo constitute one of history's most notorious exceptions. This, after all, is the city mentioned in the biblical legend of the prophet Abraham, where a Jewish community lived and thrived since Roman times, and where Jews were protected by *dhimmi* laws for centuries of Muslim rule as fellow "People of the Book." So renowned was it as a center of Jewish scholarship by the 1300s that it was chosen to house the most authoritative manuscript of the Hebrew Bible, in a majestic synagogue that stands on a foundation purportedly laid by a general of King David. As roots go, they don't get much deeper than that.

By the turn of the twentieth century, however, those roots were being pulled up. Political and economic deterioration of the Ottoman Empire in the late 1800s encouraged large numbers of Jews to leave Aleppo and cities throughout the Middle East for America, Europe, South America and other places that offered prospects of financial advancement and religious freedom.

By this time, Jewish migration to all corners of the world was reaching epic levels. Increasingly violent, government-instigated pogroms forced hundreds of thousands of Jews to flee the *shtetls,* the small Jewish towns and villages of Russia, Poland, and other Eastern European countries.

At about the same time, a Swiss Jew named Theodor Herzl launched the modern Zionist movement, motivated by the belief that Jews would never find safety in assimilation

Theodor Herzl, founder of the modern Zionist movement.

From 1882 until World War I temporarily ended immigration, the Jewish population in the British-controlled territory of Palestine grew from twenty-five thousand to perhaps a hundred thousand.

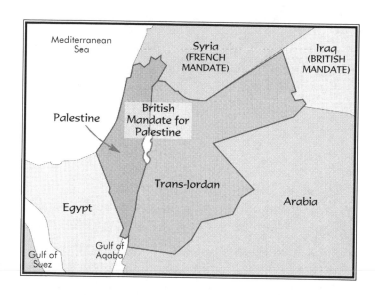

but instead needed a nation of their own to be free from anti-Semitism and gain political power.

When negotiations with the Sultan of Turkey for land in Palestine failed, he went next to the German government and finally the British. Then in 1917, Britain issued the Balfour Declaration, endorsing the creation of a Jewish homeland in Palestine.

By that time, Jews were arriving there by the boatload. From 1882 until World War I temporarily ended immigration, the Jewish population in the British-controlled territory of Palestine grew from twenty-five thousand to perhaps a hundred thousand—settlers who bought up large plots of land, often displacing local tenant farmers, as they tried to anchor themselves in the country they hoped to make their own.

However, this influx dovetailed dangerously with frustrated Arab aspirations for self-determination in the aftermath of the Ottoman Empire. The Zionist Movement coincided with increasing Arab resentment that European promises of independence had been false, which they abruptly realized when France and England parceled the Middle East into their own "colonial protectorates." As Arabs began to see that a Jewish homeland in Palestine might be more than a pipe dream, their resistance grew. Anger over the rising plausibility of a Jewish state in an Arab realm led to ongoing riots in Palestine in the 1920s and 1930s, and heightened anti-Semitism in neighboring countries.

Then in 1939, Germany invaded Poland, launching the beginning of World War II. My father was on vacation at the time with several friends in the mountains of Lebanon. Everyone rushed home, as he recalled, "piling into train cars like cattle." Knowing some of what the Nazis had been doing to Jews in Germany, they could imagine the terrible changes that might come. Though they were a thousand miles from the war zone in Europe, that distance might not mean much in territories under European control. It was a time of tremendous uncertainty and displacement worldwide.

ભ

My grandfather had sensed the growing need to get the family out of Syria for some time. Anti-Semitism in their daily lives had not become much more overt, at least "not so obvious or so witnessed," my father said. "It's just that you sort of knew it was coming because the Arabs were beginning to ask for independence, to have the French leave Syria. And you knew once they did—well, we did not know as children, but the grown-ups knew that eventually, if they took control of the country, it would be a different country completely."

Late in 1940, midway through the school year, my grandfather came to his two oldest sons, both teenagers, with a few words that would change the lives of my father and his brother, Saleh: "You are going to China to your Uncle Joe. You will go work with him."

The decision was announced, not opened for discussion. Their father had arranged for the boys to work for his brother Joe's Shanghai business exporting handmade Chinese linens to the United States.

Dad and Saleh were in college, an extension of their Mission Laïque high school. As a secular school, where religion was not taught or discussed in the classroom, the Mission

Late in 1940, my grandfather came to his two oldest sons and said, "You are going to China to your Uncle Joe. You will go work with him."

Laïque was somewhat removed from religious tensions, but Dad assumes that his father sensed more of a pro-Arab, anti-Jewish movement in his business dealings with Muslim customers than teens picked up on the street.

Yet his father also knew that getting the family out would not be quick or easy. Joe and his brother Jack had left for the United States several years earlier, as young, single men. They had started businesses and families in New York and obtained American citizenship. My grandfather had had the option to move with them but chose not to; Dad speculates that his father had an independent nature and preferred to work and travel on his own rather than with his younger brothers. By that winter of 1940, with several children and a wholesale business in Aleppo, my grandfather knew it was completely unfeasible to leave Syria on his own and send for the family later. Moving his family all at once would have been equally prohibitive financially—even if they could have gotten papers to do so.

My grandfather chose the path—in my Uncle Elie's poignant phrase—of "exporting his sons."

"The waiting list of people from Syria asking for visas to enter the U.S. was a mile long," Dad recalled, "with priorities for farmers, technicians—someone who would be productive in the United States, rather than someone coming here to go to school or work for a living."

So with political dynamics changing daily in the Arab world and the unthinkable already becoming reality in Europe, my grandfather recognized the imperative to find new options. He chose the path—in my Uncle Elie's poignant phrase—of "exporting his sons."

My grandfather's brother Joe had an importing business in New York that involved buying handmade linens from China and elsewhere in the Far East and selling them in the United States. Dad and Saleh would help Joe in his Shanghai office and—if all went as planned—use this as their stepping stone to America.

Throughout his years in Aleppo, my dad had never worked in the office of his father's textile business. "My father wanted his children to be professionals," he explained, "say, a dentist or a doctor. Education was of the utmost importance to him. When it came time for me to go to college, I told my father I wanted to be an accountant. He did not like the idea. He nixed it," Dad said with a tinge of sadness but also respect. "I'm very good at figures; math has always attracted me, and I thought being an accountant would be something I would like to do. But once he told me he didn't like it, I just discarded the idea and kept on with other studies." In hindsight, he realized that his father did not want his sons to become financially bound to Aleppo, as he himself was, but to remain free to establish themselves elsewhere.

With much of Europe at war and Japan occupying the Manchurian region of northern China, this was far from the ideal time for such a trip. But my grandfather recognized that the opportunity was better than any other that had come along, and he seized it. No one could guess how long it might be before a better prospect would appear.

CB

Dad and Saleh did not return to the Mission Laïque in January when school resumed after the winter vacation but instead began preparing for the journey. Their father arranged to escort his two oldest sons by train to Port Said, Egypt, where they would board a ship for Shanghai. Just how old were they? The account I heard most often growing up was that Dad left Aleppo when he was nineteen, yet the passport applications that his father filled out for his sons gave a birth-date of 1924 for my father and 1926 for Saleh—indicating ages of just seventeen and fifteen! Dad emphasized that exact days and years of birth were not significant in Syria when he was growing up, and the tendency to accept what one's father said was deeply ingrained. Perhaps there was some official reason which Dad never knew that his father needed to shave two years off his eldest sons' ages, or perhaps the selection of a birthdate was just arbitrary. In any case, my father formally adopted the birthdate on his passport: January 1, 1924.

How faraway and exotic China must have seemed,

Their father arranged to escort his two oldest sons by train to Port Said, Egypt, where they would board a ship for Shanghai.

decades before television, the Internet, or Google Earth! Family members and books consistently describe Aleppo at the time as provincial, and its Jewish community as insular and clannish. My father had been away from home only once, for that weeklong vacation with friends in Lebanon in the summer of 1939. He had grown up on home-cooked, strictly kosher meals and closely held traditions. Their father had intentionally kept them out of his importing business so they would not have financial obligations tying them to Syria. Now they would be working across the world in their uncle's exporting business without even the benefit of their father nearby to help.

"We really did not anticipate exactly what was going to happen," Dad explained. "We did not know anything about Shanghai. Nothing at all. In fact, we did not even know what our uncle looked like."

The absence of expectation may actually have made it easier for my father and his brother to jump into the new situation with open minds.

"We had no idea what Uncle Joe did," my father said, "nor did we know what we were expected to do. All we knew was that plans were being made to take a ship from Port Said to Shanghai, where we were to meet Uncle Joe and, hopefully, one day get to the USA."

Their next-youngest brother, Elie, on the other hand, recalled great anxiety watching his two older brothers prepare to leave.

"Their departure left a vacuum at home," he remembered, "because they were the oldest but also because they now symbolized the realization of my parents' notion of exporting sons." Elie's concern no doubt stemmed in part from recognition that—if all went according to plan—he would be the next one "exported."

My father, meanwhile, prepared to leave with a sense not of sadness or foreboding, nor of foreshadowing that this would be the last time he would see Aleppo, but of anticipation. "For young men, it was like an adventure. It's exciting when you're a teen-ager and you're going overseas, especially

"We really did not anticipate exactly what was going to happen," Dad explained. "We did not know anything about Shanghai. Nothing at all. In fact, we did not even know what our uncle looked like."

to someone who is related." After all, they had watched many other young men go abroad, returning a few years later "with piles of money and stories to tell." Friends and family joined to see them off as they walked the few blocks from their house to the railroad station.

And how might their mother have felt seeing her two oldest sons depart for an unknown city thousands of miles away? These were the boys, after all, whom she had brought back to Turkey barely a decade earlier after a month in their grand-mother's house because she could not bear to have her little boys so far from home. I suspect she simply deferred to her husband, some fifteen years her senior, in such major decisions. She surely understood the practical and political necessity of sending her sons off in search of a place with better prospects for success and survival as Jews. The house full of younger chil-dren may have buffered the pain of seeing off her oldest sons. But still, I can hardly imagine her mix of sorrow, grief, hope, anxiety, and forbearance as she watched two of her sons, such beautiful and such different young men, board a train across the desert, toward a boat that would take them across the world. I marvel today at the personal sacrifice and courage be-hind this woman's willingness to send off her two oldest sons as young men in search of a place where the family could find the freedom and safety that were fast disappearing at home.

☙

Selim Sutton and his sons set off together from Aleppo to Jerusalem, in what was then British-controlled Palestine. They spent a few days visiting family there before connecting with a train to Egypt.

Then, somewhere between Jerusalem and Egypt, the con-ductor passed through the train car checking tickets and identification papers.

"You do not have the proper papers to go to Egypt," he declared.

"What do you mean," my grandfather replied. "It's all there."

> I marvel today at the personal sacrifice and courage behind my grandmother's willingness to send off her two oldest sons as young men in search of a place where the family could find the freedom and safety that were fast disappearing at home.

" 'No,' " my father recalled the conductor saying. " 'You're lacking this or that . . . .' It was at that point that we felt anti-Semitism asserting itself." The conductor had noted in their papers that they were Jewish, and without further explanation pulled the brake cord and stopped the train in the middle of the desert, ordering my grandfather and his sons to get off. They picked up their luggage and disembarked between stations in a tiny village near the Egyptian border.

My grandfather inquired and found a driver to help them cross into Egypt and get to Port Said. But before long, a sandstorm kicked up, and the road disappeared under the blowing sand. The driver would go a short way and the car would get stuck in the sand. He would back up, try again, and get stuck again.

"Finally," Dad said, "we figured we would have to spend the night there. We were the only Jews in the whole village, I'm sure; there were no Jews at that time in that part of the world. But somehow—I don't know how—my father found somebody who could put us up for the night. They were really nice. We slept on mattresses on the floor, and the next morning, we got another cab. By that time, the road had been cleared, the sun was shining, and we got in the car and went to Egypt with no hassle, nothing—just crossed over."

Arriving in Port Said, they discovered that the delay had caused them to miss their ship to Shanghai, and the next would not sail for another two weeks. Since my grandfather could not stay away from his business that long, he left his sons in a room at a small Port Said hotel, and returned to Syria. For Dad and Saleh, it was two weeks in which they never strayed far from their little room.

"You know," my father said, "you take one step, and you never know that it's going to be a final step. I didn't know I wouldn't see [my father] again. We figured after he saw us get to the United States, he would be able to come with the rest of the family. I don't know if things would have been different had we known there was going to be a war between Japan and China, and that we would be in the middle of it."

The conductor had noted in their papers that they were Jewish, and without further explanation pulled the brake cord and stopped the train in the middle of the desert, ordering my grandfather and his sons to get off.

Bread, Boats, and Bananas

The small city of Port Said, at the mouth of the Suez Canal in the northeast corner of Egypt, lived on travel and tourism—an exotic mix for two provincial boys from Aleppo.

"At whatever time of the day a boat docked," my father recalled, "the town would come to life. All of a sudden, the lights would go on, the noises would start up, and the shops would open to receive the tourists. It was fun. There were restaurants and nightclubs. We didn't frequent the night-clubs, of course; we were young kids. This was very different from what we had seen before, completely different."

The two brothers waited alone in Port Said for two weeks. Finally, in late January, they boarded the cruiseliner *SS Conte Biancamano,* shown here in the 1930s.

"At whatever time of the day a boat docked," my father recalled, "[Port Said] would come to life," circa 1935.

Even the language was different. The people in Egypt spoke Arabic but a different dialect from that of Aleppo. "A lot of words were different," my father said. "Not such that we could not communicate"—but enough to make them feel even farther from home.

So for two weeks early in 1941, the two brothers from Aleppo waited with their tickets, not daring to explore too far from their rented room, until at last, in late January, they boarded the SS *Conte Biancamano* on a thirty-day passage to Shanghai.

"Today," Dad laughed, "to be on a thirty-day trip on an Italian ship with Italian delicacies would be the greatest thing! But in those days, for us, it was very difficult. Having never, or very rarely, had meals outside the home, the food looked foreign—and definitely not kosher! My brother and I hardly ate anything. We would sit at the dining table and eat bread and some spaghetti. Then when dinner was over, they would give us bread and cheese for dessert. That was about all that was familiar to us. We would take some of that, or some breakfast, which was bread, jam, and cheese, and leave it in the cabin for when we got hungry."

His brother's company may have helped my father some

on the journey, though by his account, he and Saleh were never particularly close. Back in Syria, each had his own group of friends. Although they were in the same grade in school, two years' age difference is significant for teens with different interests and temperaments. My father played soccer as a teen, but his friends were generally older, while Saleh's were close to his own age. Saleh was handsome and outgoing, with a gregarious personality and a happy-go-lucky sense of humor. My father seems to have been more serious—introverted by nature and laden with the responsibilities of being the oldest son. In photos, Saleh flashes a broad, engaging smile. Dad looks more studious, introspective, and conscientious. It probably did not help that their parents placed different expectations on the boys—his mother being stricter with Dad (the "head of the fish"), his father harsher on Saleh.

My father remembers Aden, Yemen, as sunny, dry, and extremely hot, even though the trip took place in winter, circa 1936.

℃

The *Conte Biancamano* sailed down the Suez Canal, across the Red Sea, and around the Arabian Peninsula, making its first stop at Aden, in Yemen, south of Saudi Arabia's southern

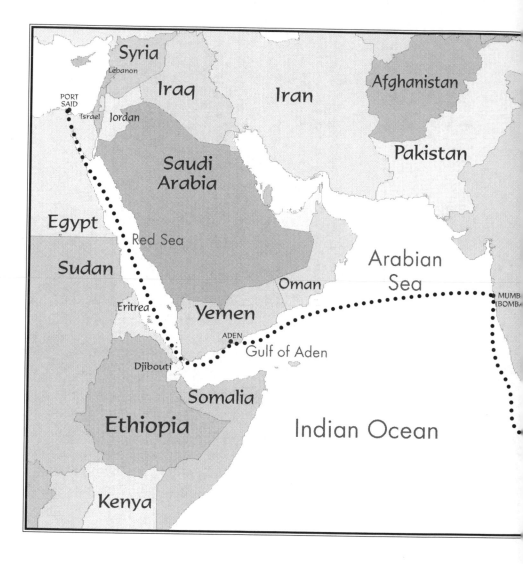

The brothers' journey from Port Said, Egypt, to Shanghai, China, aboard the SS Conte Biancamano took 30 days.

tip. My father remembers it as sunny, dry, and extremely hot—like virtually every port on the journey through the tropics, even though the trip took place in winter.

"The boat trip was a learning and discovering experience," Dad said. After Aden, the next stop was Bombay, in India [Mumbai these days]. "It was a densely populated city, and streets were crowded and filthy. Poverty was rampant. We shopped some and even had a haircut at a barbershop. Whatever prompted us to take a haircut in Bombay, I'll never know! Anyway, it felt adventuresome."

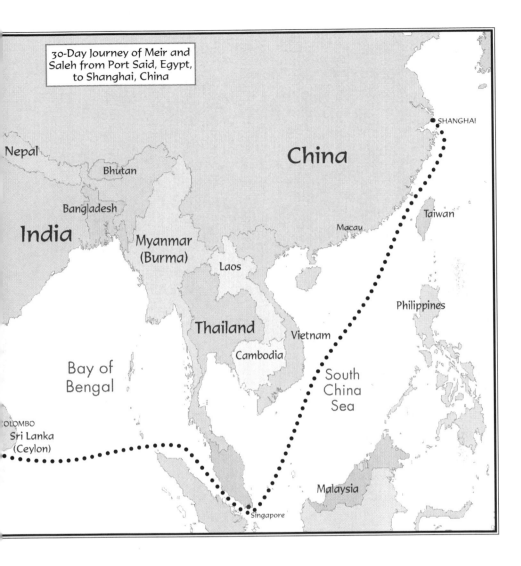

30-Day Journey of Meir and Saleh from Port Said, Egypt, to Shanghai, China

On a hillside on the city's outskirts, they saw piles of dead bodies laid over iron bars in the open air, with vultures flying overhead and feeding on the remains. When they were picked clean, the bones fell through the bars. "We figured that this was the cheapest way to dispose of the dead versus burial or cremation," my father said. ADD: What the brothers didn't know was that they were witnessing was a Zoroastrian burial ritual, something they had never seen in Aleppo.

From Bombay, the ship sailed to Colombo on the island of Ceylon, a British colony off the coast of India, which is

Bombay was a densely populated city, and streets were crowded and filthy. Poverty was rampant, early 1900s.

now the independent nation of Sri Lanka. When it docked, local people sailed out on small boats, shouting up to the deck about what goods they had for sale. Passengers would throw coins, and young children would dive into the water to catch them. My father and Saleh, still eager to find foods they could eat, bought a huge stalk of bananas that they took back to their cabin! They had not considered abandoning their Orthodox upbringing.

When the ship docked in Singapore, the Pacific Ocean was so calm that it seemed to my father they could get off and walk across it. At last, at the end of February 1941, they arrived at their final port of call: Shanghai. Even from the deck, they could see it was the biggest city they had ever seen.

"We were overwhelmed," Dad said.

My Moon Rivers

n September 2000, my parents and I visited China on a three-week tour arranged through an American travel company. By then I was deep into interviews and research about my father's experiences, and jumped at the chance to augment verbal pictures with a few live ones. To help my twelve-year-old son Ariel—

My parents and me at the Huxinting Teahouse, Yuyuan Garden, in Shanghai, 2000.

and myself—come to terms with the journey, I poked a tooth-pick in a plum to signify where we were, rotated it halfway around and stuck in another to show where I was going.

Mom, Dad, and I landed in Hong Kong a few days before our tour started, to give ourselves time to adjust to jetlag. We spent three nights at the Peninsula Hotel, where Dad had stayed on business trips after World War II. In 2000, just a year after the British turnover of Hong Kong to China, the Peninsula Hotel still felt like a vestige of the old Empire. Elegantly dressed women sipped Darjeeling in the hotel restaurants, poured for them from silver teapots by deferential waiters. (When I carelessly placed my silver tea strainer on my butter plate one morning instead of its special silver platter, a waiter briskly moved it to its proper place.) Each night my father left his leather shoes in a little cubicle by our hotel room door, also accessible by key from the corridor. In the morning the shoes would be back in the cubicle, shined and buffed by the diminutive Chinese porter assigned to our floor. But for the beeper on our chambermaid's waist and the fax machine in our room, we could have been in another century and political epoch.

One morning Mom had a fitting for a suit by a traditional Chinese tailor, in a small store on the hotel's mezzanine. In the lobby below us, a piano, flute, and cello trio played "Moon River" for guests. (By the end of our trip, we would have heard that song in no fewer than three hotel lobbies throughout China. Did something in that Andy Williams chestnut, the background music of my 1960s suburban childhood, epitomize America to a country newly emerging to the Western world? Or did international tourists and business-people on the cusp of the twenty-first century still resonate nostalgically with the song's "drifters, off to see the world"?)

After a few days exploring Hong Kong on our own, we loaded our luggage into a taxi that took us across the channel to the Mandarin Oriental Hotel, where our tour would begin the next day. Too tired and hot for more sightseeing, we stretched out on beds in one of our two adjacent hotel rooms and watched TV. Dad found an American channel showing

In the lobby below us, a piano, flute, and cello trio played "Moon River" for guests.

a documentary on (who else!) Andy Williams. Williams explained to the interviewer, a little sheepishly, that he almost rejected Henry Mancini's "Moon River" as too corny when he first heard it; the words "huckleberry friend" especially rankled his ears. Somehow he was persuaded to record the song that would be associated with him forever after, he explained, grinning proudly. I smiled, too. Across the world from my husband and son, in a fancy hotel with my parents, I found myself in an oddly comforting warp of time and space.

Those idle hours in the hotel room after revisiting places he had not seen in decades stirred Dad's memories of living in China during the war. Stretched out on the bed on that muggy September afternoon in his neatly creased Gap pants and cotton pullover, with an arm propped behind his head, his buffed Florsheim loafers tucked under the bed, he recalled how a year into the war, the Japanese confiscated radiators from everyone's homes and offices in Shanghai so they could melt down the steel for tanks and other weapons. He wore silk long underwear night and day during Shanghai's damp, cold winters from then until the end of the war.

Revisiting places he had not seen in decades stirred Dad's memories of living in China during World War. II. "War changes you," he said, "and as time goes on, it changes you more." Japanese soldiers are shown here marching into Shanghai on December 7, 1941.

Dad recalled an air raid drill in which a young European man insisted on going through a barricade, attempting to persuade the Japanese soldiers of his need to get where he was going, but the soldiers knocked him to the ground and beat him. Dad froze in place for fear of provoking soldiers who did not understand a word of his language and who took all Westerners as a potential threat.

"War changes you, doesn't it?" I asked, an awareness dawning.

"War changes you," Dad said, "and as time goes on, it changes you more."

I had always assumed that our family, by the grace of geography and political alliances, had escaped direct impact of the war that so devastated the Jewish people. My father's tendency to downplay past adversities and look ahead only fed that assumption. But in that hotel room, a few hundred miles from where he passed the war years alone, I imagined a young man across the world from, and virtually out of communication with, his family, honing his resources to cope with escalating deprivation and uncertainty. How the events we live through will end is always a mystery until they can be viewed through the hindsight of history.

> I had always assumed that our family, by the grace of geography and political alliances, had escaped direct impact of the war that so devastated the Jewish people.

"We knew all the Japanese had to do was give in to the Germans' demand to release all the Jews in their occupation area, and then God knows—they would probably take us to Europe and put us in a concentration camp and so forth. But thank God the Japanese were not falling for that; they were saying, these are our people, under our control, and we make the decisions. But at that time, we really did not know what they would do. We were scared stiff."

Off to see the world, Andy Williams sang, *there's such a lot of world to see.* How much more was there to see in my own family?

New City, New Names

hen the *Conte Biancamano* docked in Shanghai Harbor in February 1941, my father and his brother waited in their cabin for their uncle to meet them. They had sent Joe a telegram from the ship telling him their arrival date and cabin number. From the deck outside the cabin, Dad and Saleh watched hundreds of people greeting friends and disembarking. Although they had never seen a photo of their uncle, my father somehow spotted him among the crowd by the strong family resemblance— perhaps the same high, wide brow and dark eyes so prominent in my father and his brothers today. Still, they waited

The world-famous Bund and harbor, Shanghai, China, much as it looked when Meïr and Saleh arrived in 1941.

in their cabin until their uncle came up to meet them, so as not to lose one another in the crowd.

"My uncle was very surprised by us," Dad said. "You see, he had no idea how old I was or Saleh was. My father was older than Joe. However, apparently he forgot that he got married before my father, so my brother and I were no older than his children. He must have thought we had been in business with my father, but when he saw us, he realized that we were not businesspeople at all, just recent students."

Their uncle took them straight to the YMCA on Nanjing Road, where he had reserved two small rooms. Just the first of many changes they encountered in the new city was a new name for each of them. Joe shortened Saleh's name to the more-American "Sal" (though his family at home still often called him Saleh). Meïr, my father, would be forever after known as "Mike." Insignificant changes, perhaps, in a city of refugees but representative of the forces of displacement and reidentification that shaped Shanghai.

Since 1842, Shanghai had been one of China's five "international cities"—ports opened to economic development by the Treaty of Nanjing at the end of the first Opium War with Britain. The treaty aimed to facilitate outside investment in China, originally through trade in opium but later tea and other commodities. First Britain, then America and France, were granted foreign "concessions"—autonomous districts within these cities where the countries maintained their own police, banks, businesses, churches, and governing councils. So for a hundred years, people seeking economic opportunities had been coming to Shanghai from all over Europe, the Middle East, India, and the Far East.

Long before Dad and Sal arrived, the American and British concessions had merged into the Shanghai International Settlement, which contained the city's main commercial and entertainment establishments. Boats docked at the edge of this district in the harbor of the Huangpu River, and

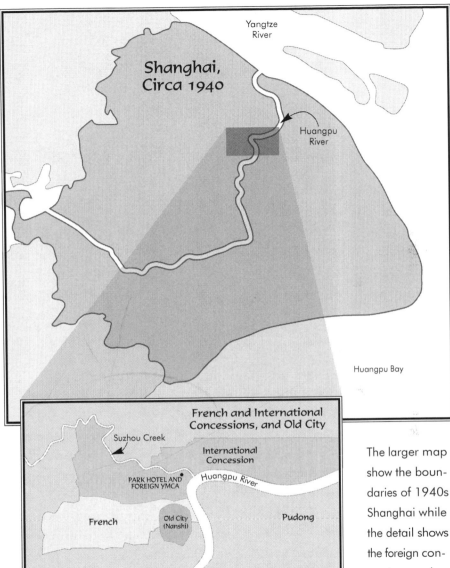

Shanghai,
Circa 1940

Yangtze
River

Huangpu
River

Huangpu Bay

French and International
Concessions, and Old City

Suzhou Creek

International
Concession

PARK HOTEL AND
FOREIGN YMCA

Huangpu River

French

Old City
(Nanshi)

Pudong

The larger map show the boundaries of 1940s Shanghai while the detail shows the foreign concessions and Old City.

major international businesses lined the Bund, the wide avenue abutting the river. Many Americans lived just across the river in the Hongkou district.

The French Concession, primarily residential, had the lovely tree-lined avenues and elegant Art Deco architecture that earned pre-war Shanghai its nickname of "The Paris of the East." Many of the city's "White Russians"—non-

One of seven Jewish temples in Shanghai, Beth Ahron Synagogue typified the Art Deco style that earned pre-war Shanghai its nickname of "The Paris of the East."

Communists who had fled the Bolshevik Revolution in 1917—also settled there.

Finally, there was the large portion of the city still under Chinese jurisdiction. One could commit a crime in one part of the city and find immunity just by crossing into another. Going from one concession to another, with their changes of architectural styles and even the language on street signs, must have felt a bit like a chapter from Lewis Carroll.

What a stunning contrast to Aleppo's Old World, provincial pace! Shanghai in the mid-twentieth century was a kind of nexus of diaspora, where people came from all over the world, recreating themselves by combinations of choice and fate. It was a way station between old and new identities. Distinctions between insider and outsider dissolved. Dad's passport from that time bears no stamp for Shanghai, because entry required no documentation of any kind. As an international city, Shanghai belonged to everyone and no one; it accepted anyone, regardless of origin,

requiring no proof, permission, or identification. It was the epitome of opportunity and abandon.

From left to right, Shanghai's Park Hotel, Foreign YMCA, and China United Apartments, circa 1938.

☙

Joe retained a room at the Park Hotel on Nanjing Road for his business trips to Shanghai. My dad and Saleh—now Mike and Sal—had rooms at the YMCA just next door. Though there were no kitchen facilities, the building had a restaurant, exercise room, and indoor swimming pool. Joe's office was also on Nanjing Road, several blocks closer to downtown. The two young men would work in the office every day until four o'clock, then meet some of Joe's friends for tea in the lobby of the nearby Cathay Hotel, on the Bund.

Joe set about the task of training his nephews in the workings of Sutton and Husney Importers and Exporters. The business involved selecting and purchasing hand-embroidered linens unique to the Chinese towns and villages

Joe's manager, a Syrian-Jewish man from Brooklyn named Ed Betesh, took care of the office when Joe was out of the country.

where they were sewn and preparing them for export to the United States. Some were bought from vendors who came to the office with samples. Others were made to order from custom patterns and designs or bought on trips to surrounding towns and villages. Joe had a manager named Ed Betesh, a Syrian-Jewish man from Brooklyn, who took care of the office when Joe was out of the country. In addition, two Chinese brothers translated with the vendors, and a few women inspected and packed the goods for shipment to the United States.

Just a few weeks after my father and his brother arrived, Joe decided to send Sal to the tiny fishing village of Swatow in southeastern China on an extended stay to set up a new office for the business—seemingly assuming that Sal, the more-outgoing brother, was the older. Thus, soon after stepping off the *Conte Biancamano*, Sal was on another boat, this time on his own, heading several hundred miles down the South China Sea to a little town north of Hong Kong.

Shanghai was hardly sanitary at the time by modern American standards, but Dad describes Swatow (which he visited after the war) as much worse, with raw sewage flowing down the streets. Sal returned to Shanghai a few months later weak and pale. My father took him to a doctor, who X-rayed his chest and diagnosed Sal with tuberculosis.

Actually he may have contracted the disease back in Syria and just manifested symptoms during his time in Swatow. A few years earlier, his mother's younger brother had come down with tuberculosis in Aleppo. "Mother moved her brother from the dingy room where he was living into our apartment so he could be more comfortable," Dad said. "I don't know why she did this with small children in the house, knowing the disease was highly contagious, but he lived with us for a few months until he died." Tuberculosis can, in fact, lay dormant for years and not emerge until the immune system has been weakened for some other reason. Dad sent a telegram telling his father that Sal's condition had worsened and Joe thought he should return to Aleppo to be taken care of at home.

And so Sal went back to Syria, alone, in the spring of 1941. Elie, who still lived in Aleppo and eagerly awaited his brother's return, describes the return trip as much more arduous than the journey to Shanghai just a few months before: "The war, with its mounting battles and complications around the globe, made getting a visa next to impossible. Reserving transportation was made difficult by overbookings and long delays. I watched my parents' anxieties heighten with each passing day. They wanted Saleh home. They wanted to give him the care he needed to get better."

Dad stayed on in Shanghai, working in his uncle's business, keeping his focus on his role in his family's move from Syria to the United States.

"My business in Shanghai was dealing with my uncle," he explained. "I liked very much that I was staying with someone who was like my father. I relied on him to tell me what to do, since I had not been in business before. I didn't know what else to feel. And remember that as long as the war was not in the Far East, I thought I could go back to Aleppo at any time, and then return to Shanghai, or do whatever my family needed me to do. I really did not have any way to figure it out and weigh it all as to how long or how difficult it was going to be."

�❧

Among the many nationalities in Shanghai at the time—Chinese, Japanese, Russian, French, British, American, Iranian, Iraqi, Syrian, Indian, and others—English was the common language.

"It seemed that everyone either spoke English or was in the process of learning it," Dad said. "You did not even need to speak Chinese to do business in a Chinese store, since Chinese shopkeepers all had someone who could speak English for them."

Dad had studied English at school in Aleppo but was far from fluent. "Our English teacher wanted a chance to prac-

Among the many nationalities in Shanghai at the time— Chinese, Japanese, Russian, French, British, American, Iranian, Iraqi, Syrian, Indian and others— English was the common language.

To better learn English, my dad spent many free evenings watching Robert Taylor, Clark Gable, Dorothy Lamour, Bob Hope, and other Hollywood stars in the American movies that eventually made their way to Shanghai.

tice his French, rather than teach us English," he laughed. "By the end, I could translate a page of Arabic to English or the other way around, but I could not put two words together in a sentence."

At this point, however, English became the language to know, so he practiced with new friends he met. After someone suggested that he go to American movies to immerse himself in the language, he spent many free evenings watching Robert Taylor, Clark Gable, Dorothy Lamour, Bob Hope, and other Hollywood stars fall in and out of love and get themselves in and out of trouble. These films were hardly new by the time they made their way to China, but they provided a linguistic tool as well as a peephole into American culture. Many of us remember when we first saw the Orson Welles classic *Citizen Kane*. I saw it at the Biograph Theatre, the wonderful, now-defunct repertory cinema in Georgetown. Dad saw it in Shanghai. With the aid of this cinematic crash course, he was able to understand and even converse in English within a few months.

C_B

Shanghai was hardly without a Jewish community; in fact, it had several. Jewish entrepreneurs had begun moving to China from Europe and the Middle East in the mid-1800s to help develop the newly opened "international cities." Many came from European countries that had severely restricted Jews' involvement in commerce. In the late 1700s, large numbers of Baghdadi Jews began migrating to Bombay, where they found greater freedom to conduct business and observe religious customs under British rule than they had in Iraq under Arab rule. Many of these families later moved to Shanghai for greater opportunities in this newly opened economic sphere.

The Sassoon family of Baghdad (by way of Bombay) stood at the vanguard of these Iraqi-Jewish entrepreneurs in China in the 1840s. Historian David Kranzler, in a 1998 PBS interview, compared the Sassoons to the Rothschilds, the German Jewish business magnates who amassed a fortune in the banking industry in nineteenth-century Europe. Much as the Rothschild patriarch sent his sons to establish a financial and industrial empire across Western Europe, David Sassoon sent his sons to Shanghai and other Asian cities, where they established commercial enterprises that became hugely successful.

The Sassoons would arrive in these cities with at least ten men, to ensure a *minyan* for Jewish prayers, Kranzler explained. Then when other Baghdadi Jews followed, they would be assured of a Jewish community in which to practice and people from their own culture with whom to work. The men would even study kosher slaughtering practices so they could eat meat in these new countries. Their merchant empire spanning southern Asia helped the Sassoons become one of the wealthiest families in the world.

Victor Sassoon built Shanghai's magnificent Cathay Hotel, the luxurious Gothic structure along the Bund where Dad and his uncle met friends for tea every afternoon. In the

Shanghai was hardly without a Jewish community; in fact, it had several.

The wealthy Baghdadi Jewish community of Shanghai prepared transitional shelters such as the one shown here for Jewish immigrants from Europe. Houses and apartment buildings were rebuilt into large dormitories where the refugees lived until they found jobs and could afford private lodging.

early 1940s, the Cathay was in its heyday, visited by such international politicians, entrepreneurs, and celebrities as Charlie Chaplin, Gen. George C. Marshall, George Bernard Shaw, and Noël Coward. American expatriates frequented its famed Old Jazz Bar.

Russian Jews had begun settling in Shanghai early in the twentieth century, fleeing first the pogroms and later the Bolshevik Revolution. And from 1933 to 1941, an estimated eighteen thousand to twenty thousand European Jews arrived in Shanghai seeking refuge from the Nazis.

Three fascinating documentary films, *The Port of Last Resort* (1998), *Shanghai Ghetto* (2002), and *Last Refuge: The Story of Jewish Refugees in Shanghai* (2004), recount life for these European Jews through their own reminiscences.

Dana Janklowicz-Mann, co-director with Amir Mann of *"Shanghai Ghetto,"* describes the exodus set in motion after the Nazis were elected to power in Germany in 1933: "Jewish men were being picked up and put into concentration camps. They were told, 'You have X amount of time to leave—two weeks, a month—if you can find a country that will take you.' Outside, their wives and friends were struggling to get a passport, a visa, anything to help them get out. But embassies were closing their doors all over, and countries, including the United States, were closing their borders. . . . It started as a rumor in Vienna. . . . 'There's a place you can go where you don't need a visa. They have free entry.' It just spread like fire, and whoever could went for it."

The trick was getting there. Refugees did not need a visa or other documents to enter Shanghai, but they *did* need the fare for passage there, available only on luxury liners from Italy. Steamships sailed from Genoa through the Suez Canal and across the Indian Ocean to China. Jewish refugees needed to get to Italy and purchase passage for the journey. Some received help for their ticket from the American Jewish Joint Distribution Committee and other relief organizations. The passengers described a surreal three-week journey on a luxury ship with food and entertainment, sandwiched between their escape from persecution in Germany, Austria, or Poland and arrival in a squalid ghetto in Shanghai.

The greatest numbers of these European Jewish refugees arrived in Shanghai in 1938 and 1939. Many left after Kristallnacht, the horrific night in November 1938 when hundreds of synagogues and Jewish-owned businesses throughout Germany and Austria were destroyed. But soon after Germany invaded Poland on September 1, 1939, Italy joined the war on the side of the Germans, and sea travel from Italy to Shanghai ended. Only more-arduous routes were left, including trains across Siberia and China, for the smaller number of determined refugees who still managed to get to Shanghai.

These "Shanghai Jews" were permitted to leave Germany with no more than two suitcases per person and ten marks—roughly eight U.S. dollars then—and so they arrived in Shanghai with no financial assets. The wealthy Baghdadi Jewish community of Shanghai, with help from American Jewish charities, prepared transitional shelters for them in the Hongkou district, which was still recovering from bombing

The greatest numbers of these European Jewish refugees arrived in Shanghai in 1938 and '39. Many left after Kristallnacht, the horrific night in November 1938 when hundreds of synagogues and Jewish-owned businesses throughout Germany and Austria were destroyed.

by the Japanese in 1937 in the second Sino-Japanese war. Houses and apartment buildings were rebuilt into large dormitories where the refugees lived until they found jobs and could afford private lodging.

My father and his brother had met some of those German-Jewish refugees on their voyage from Italy to Shanghai on the *Conte Biancamano.* The Germans feared that they might be exposed as Jews if they mixed with others on the ship, and in Shanghai, he recognized some of them going into a church one Sunday morning, still afraid to reveal that they were Jews, unsure how far the reach of the Nazis would extend.

These "Shanghai Jews" were permitted to leave Germany with no more than two suitcases per person and ten marks—roughly eight U.S. dollars then—and so they arrived in Shanghai with no financial assets.

CB

"Everyone you met was enjoying life in Shanghai to the fullest," Dad recalled of his first months in the new city in the spring of 1941, "never dreaming that a few months later, everything would change with Japan's entry into the war." Shanghai bustled with commerce and revelry, seemingly impervious to the conflicts intensifying around the world.

By summer, however, signs of war were inescapable. Dad's Uncle Joe got his first serious indication that China might soon be involved on a business trip to Japan in August, when he realized that Japanese authorities had ransacked his luggage in his hotel room to see if he was a spy. He knew that as an American citizen, he would be considered an enemy if Japan and the United States ended up being at war. Japan already had troops in Shanghai, although it didn't govern the city, after invading much of eastern China in 1937. In the summer of 1941, Americans began vacating the Hongkou district where they lived because they feared U.S. involvement in the war, and Japanese troops took their place.

"[The Americans] anticipated that war was coming and wanted not to stay there and be subjected to Japanese occupation," Dad explained. "That left a vacuum, and the Japan-

ese came in and filled that vacuum." Joe packed his belongings and booked passage on what turned out to be the last
passenger ship to the United States until the war was over,
leaving my father alone in Shanghai. The young man whose
father had deliberately directed him away from his textile
business in Aleppo found himself across the world from his
family, working in the linen exporting business, living in a
little room at the YMCA.

"Realizing that I was not capable of taking care of the
whole business myself, my uncle kept on a manager," Dad
explained, the Syrian man who ran the Shanghai office when
Joe was out of the country. Still, much of the responsibility
fell on my father, who felt compelled to learn what the business required as quickly as he could, although, "Of course, I
was still a young kid."

For the next few months, he continued working in the office with the manager, communicating regularly with his father and uncle by mail. He recalled the great trepidation he
felt after the Americans pulled out from Shanghai, knowing
the Japanese were allied with the Germans and that there was

Everyone you met was enjoying life in Shanghai to the fullest," recalled Dad, seated at the far left with several friends at the Shanghai Masonic Club, 1942.

Uncle Joe packed his belongings and booked passage on what turned out to be the last passenger ship to the United States until the war was over, leaving my father alone in Shanghai.

no way to foretell what they would do in Shanghai if the city became involved in the war. There was nothing to do but wait.

Uproar at the Harbor

ne Sunday night in early December, after an evening out with friends, my father returned to his room at the YMCA and was startled by an uproar from the harbor.

"Late that Sunday night," he said, "maybe already early Monday morning, I heard a great commotion, the sound of bombing and shooting. I got up, put on my topcoat, and went up to the roof, together with several other people in the YMCA. We saw fire and smoke in the distance by the harbor."

From the roof, they witnessed the very first moments that the war reached China.

Earlier that day—December 7, 1941—my father had heard on his shortwave radio that the Japanese had bombed the U.S. naval fleet in Pearl Harbor, Hawaii, outside Honolulu. "The American and British soldiers had vacated Shanghai," he said, "leaving only a small force to guard the embassies. In Shanghai harbor, there were two small warships, one British and one American. When the bombing of Pearl Harbor took place, the Japanese forces in Shanghai demanded that the British and Americans surrender these boats. The Americans surrendered right away, realizing there was no sense in fighting the [Japanese] army with just a handful of Marines. They were all taken prisoner. The British did not want to surrender, and the Japanese hit the ship and took it anyway."

People up on the YMCA roof witnessed this bombing and gunfire in the harbor in the middle of the night. The next morning, they watched from office windows as the Japanese

In Shanghai harbor, there were two small warships, one British and one American. When the bombing of Pearl Harbor took place, the Japanese forces in Shanghai demanded that the British and Americans surrender these boats.

army marched across the bridge over the Huangpu River from the Hongkou district to the main commercial areas.

Shanghai was thus occupied by the Japanese from the first day of the war in the Pacific. The routines my father had established, working for the business while keeping in long-distance contact with his uncle in New York and family in Aleppo, came to an abrupt halt.

"As soon as the war broke out," he said, "everything stopped completely. No more exporting. No ships were allowed to leave, because Japan and the United States were at war. Everyone had to fend for himself and make his own living."

In less than a year, my dad had gone from living at home and attending school to living on his own across the world in a country at war.

In less than a year, he had gone from living at home and attending school to living on his own across the world in a country at war. "But if anything matures you," he said, "it's being on your own to fend for yourself, with nobody to rely on for anything. That's when your resources become the surviving factor."

Perhaps those months were more fraught with anxiety than he remembered through the foreshortening lens of memory, but in hindsight, it seemed that practicality—as it probably always had all his life—held sway over sentimentality.

"At the back of your mind, you know that it doesn't help to feel one way or the other about it, because there's no ship, there's no train, there's nothing that can take you back to your family. I suppose it changed the responsibility I experienced, from what I had to do to please my mother—setting an example for the younger brothers and sister; that's a pressure in itself—to something else. At that point, it became financial. Luckily, I had enough sense to do some business that kept me earning enough money to live on."

With international commerce shut down, business opportunities shifted to identifying items that might turn a profit during wartime. To wit: sewing needles.

Sewing needles!

"During a war," Dad explained, "people speculate on different things that, out of scarceness, go up in price. People do not want to keep cash, because it loses value as the war goes

on. They just try to buy anything that they think will go up in value. I heard that there was business being done in sewing needles, which were in demand as a means for people to invest their money rather than keep it in Chinese dollars. You see, the Chinese were known worldwide for their embroidery, and during the war, they were not making sewing needles because they were using the steel for weapons." Any needles one could find therefore would become increasingly valuable.

"I had a few dollars saved, so I went to a Chinaman who was dealing in sewing needles. I said I wanted to buy five cases. We decided on a price, but I didn't have enough money to buy them. Whatever money I had, I put down as a deposit and said I'd take delivery within a week. I tried to peddle them the first day, the second day, and all of a sudden maybe about the fourth or fifth day, while going to lunch, a man I knew in the Syrian community tapped me on the shoulder and said, 'I hear you have five cases of sewing needles you want to sell. How much do you want for them?' I told him the price, he agreed, and he paid me for them. I picked them up, paid for them, and put a deposit down for *ten* cases. So the same thing happened; I just kept selling them and buying more. The next thing I knew, anybody that wanted sewing needles was told, 'Go and see Mike Sutton. He has sewing needles!'"

The night of December 7, 1941, my dad was awakened by the sounds of bombing and shooting. He got up, put on his topcoat, and went up to the roof, together with several other people in the YMCA. They were witness to the Japanese bombing of British and American ships in the Huangpu River—the very first moments that the war reached China.

Sal back in
Aleppo with his
parents, circa
1945.

ℭ

   Sal, returning home to Aleppo, sadly discovered that it was not as easy to travel in a world at war as it had been several months before. His initial trip from Port Said to Shanghai with my father had meant a month on an Italian cruise ship, with passage arranged by their father. The return voyage took several months, involving numerous delays and complicated rerouting around countries engaged in the escalating war. When at last he reached Port Said, his father made another trip to Egypt, this time to pick up his son—now weak, listless, and wracked with coughing spasms—and bring him back home.

   Elie remembers the return of a much-changed older brother. "At home, all of us saw how very sick Saleh was. A continuous fever rendered him lethargic, and he only wanted to sleep. Coughing spasms shook his skeletal frame, and sharp pains stabbed into his chest. Sometimes I sat with him and watched as he spit up blood." Their father found Saleh a sanitarium in the mountains of Lebanon, which placed him under strict medical supervision. "If he had remained and completed his course of treatment," Elie said, "he would have been cured. But Saleh had no tolerance for isolation and no patience to wait out the recovery time."

My grandfather had decided long before not to allow his sons to earn a living in Syria so as not to be economically bound to the country. So after returning to Aleppo from the sanitarium, Saleh had to pass his time in a leisurely and surely boring way for such a vibrant, outgoing young man. He made clear that he wanted to return to Shanghai when he could.

Everyone—including Saleh himself—knew the grave risk this would pose to his health, but by then, they were all convinced of the imperative to get out of Syria at any cost. "Saleh's desires were risky," Elie explained, "but times were very different then. Whether my parents' concerns were deemed as acts of desperation in light of his health or the world around us is not something I can justify accurately. Would they have otherwise taken a course of action that would be considered foolish under normal circumstances? The fact is that we were not living in ordinary times. We were Jews, living in a hostile country."

♋

In Shanghai, my father continued to buy and sell what he could to make enough money to survive. The legal currency after the Japanese occupation remained the Chinese yuan, but many people traded yuan for foreign currency with a stronger value. People who earned wages in yuan often converted them into the much-healthier American dollar. Other people needed to convert American dollars to yuan for living expenses or other everyday items. My father got into the business of trading currencies from seller to buyer, charging a broker's commission.

One man he knew bought "thousands upon thousands" of Hong Kong dollars, which had been severely depreciated after the Japanese seized control from Great Britain, and traded for about 20 percent of face value. No one knew whether, once

In Shanghai, my father continued to buy and sell what he could to make enough money to survive.

the war was over, the British would honor the Hong Kong dollars that the Japanese had floated in the market for their own use. But this man speculated that the British eventually would regain control of Hong Kong and restore the currency. He was right! When the war ended, the British immediately declared that all Hong Kong money in circulation would be honored dollar for dollar. The man made a fortune.

☙

My father remembers himself as being devoutly observant as a child and young man.

My father remembers himself as being devoutly observant as a child and young man. "From the day I was bar mitzvahed until the day I left to go to Shanghai, I used to say that my *tefillin* never saw the house, because I kept it at the synagogue and used to pray there every morning." On the boat trip to Shanghai, he and his brother kept kosher even when it meant eating little more than bread and bananas.

Living alone in Shanghai, separated from family and a Jewish community, these practices grew harder to maintain.

"In Syria, the routine was set," he explained. "Men in business would come home for lunch in the middle of the day. Children would come home from school to eat together. It was easy to miss school on Saturdays to observe the Sabbath, because so many other Jewish children were doing the same."

By this time, the city he lived in had thousands of "Shanghai Jews" who had fled Nazi Europe, primarily in the Hongkou section and the French concession. A Sephardic community from India, Iraq, and Iran had built a large synagogue on Bubbling Well Road, not far from where my father lived, but their customs differed significantly from Aleppo's. Most of the Syrian men my father met in Shanghai had their own families with whom they celebrated holidays and the Sabbath. They might invite him home for a Friday night dinner now and then, but he was not enveloped in a large family and larger community that observed, ate, and celebrated together as he had been in Aleppo.

In Syria, he explained, observing Jewish rituals and teach-ings went hand in glove with belonging to a Jewish community. The rabbi would give interpretations of biblical stories and reasons behind the customs they followed. Accepting those explanations was one element of considering oneself Jewish. The other was practicing traditions in the company of family and friends. To his eyes, the religious understanding that he acquired in school and at home was more figurative than literal: "Did it *actually* take the Jews forty years to cross the desert, or just one or two? That was not the important issue," he said. What mattered were the messages and morals *within* the stories, and the context of community observance.

Outside such context, living on his own, sustaining these practices was difficult. Even when his uncle still lived in Shanghai, Dad was surprised to find that Joe did not particularly care whether the meat he ate was kosher. Initially, Dad kept kosher and said prayers regularly, but these practices gradually tapered off.

"Of course, if you were cooking every meal at home, you could make sure you had kosher meat," he said, "but in restaurants, there was no kosher food. So little by little, I just adapted. At first, it was difficult. It was with a little trepidation at first, but then I began to lift the taboo and start eating. But I was still being careful—by careful I mean no pork or ham, no shellfish like shrimps or clams."

Letting go of these practices for the first time in his life does not seem to have been accompanied by a crisis of faith or sense of guilt. It did not mean letting go of his Jewish identity or renouncing a belief in God. Rather it was a response to extraordinary circumstances—a reflection of a practical streak deep within my father's nature. "Little by little," he said, "it just wore off."

Initially, Dad kept kosher and said prayers regularly, but these practices gradually tapered off.

CB

For the first year after Japan seized Shanghai in December 1941, daily life in the city did not change tremendously. Initially—when the Japanese were doing well in the war—con-

As the Japanese marched through Southeast Asia, taking control of China, Hong Kong, Singapore, the Philippines, and many other territories, my father kept up by listening to a shortwave radio in his room at the Y. The surrender of American troops to the Japanese in the Philippines in 1942 is shown here.

trol over Shanghai was loose. In the first months of the war in the Pacific, the Japanese marched through Southeast Asia, taking control of China, Hong Kong, Singapore, the Philippines, Malaya, Indonesia, the Dutch East Indies, and other small islands. Residents of Shanghai could move about the city at will. My father listened to Arabic music and kept up with news from around the world on a shortwave radio in his room at the Y. He picked up broadcasts from the Middle East, England, France—even reports of the war from the Nazi perspective broadcast in Arabic by a German station.

Almost a year into the war, however—once the news was no longer consistently in Japan's favor—Japanese authorities required everyone first to register their shortwave radios, and later to surrender them. From then until the war's end, virtually the only information about the war came from hearsay and Japanese propaganda. "The rumors circulated a lot, about where every battle was and what happened," Dad said.

With his radiator seized to melt down for weapons, Dad remained bundled up in long underwear under his clothes all winter and slept under a heavy blanket in flannel pajamas and a sweater. With no heat even in emergency shelters, homeless people froze to death on the streets. Every day the newspapers reported the number of people who had died on the streets the night before.

In the second year of occupation, the Japanese set up camps for British and American citizens. "These were not concentration camps as we know them from Germany and Europe," Dad explained. "These were detention camps. They would take a large warehouse or school that was not being used and put anybody in them who was British or American. They housed them there until the end of the war." The detainees included citizens of India and other British territories, and any remaining Americans. His Uncle Joe, with American citizenship, would have been one of those detainees had he not foreseen the coming of war in time to return to the States.

My father was fortunate not to be relocated to these camps. By the vagaries of colonial politics, he had French citizenship, since Syria was a French protectorate. The Japanese considered the Vichy government of occupied France, which had surrendered to German occupation in 1940, as the "Friendly French." The oppositional government of Charles de Gaulle was in exile in London. Anyone with French papers therefore was not considered an enemy of the Japanese and could roam the city without restrictions. No one was permitted to leave the city, however, regardless of papers— though, as Dad recalled, they would not have felt safe doing so anyway in a time of war.

Dad knew men who were relocated to these detention centers, including an Iraqi friend—a British subject who was an engineer. He figured out how to build a small shortwave radio so inconspicuous that he kept it hidden in his room throughout the war, letting him pick up news reports from all over the world which he shared with his friends. "You would never

No one was permitted to leave Shanghai, regardless of papers— though, as Dad recalled, they would not have felt safe doing so anyway in a time of war.

know it was a radio," Dad said. "It just looked like a small box. The Japanese never knew he had it. If they did, who knows? It was risky, but then again, they were not that well organized and didn't keep track of everything that went on."

༄

In late 1942, the Nazis stepped up pressure on the Japanese to turn over the Shanghai Jews. The Japanese, however, refused to bow to Nazi pressure to hand over the Jews, and instead confined them in a restricted zone—back in Hongkou.

In late 1942, the Nazis stepped up pressure on the Japanese to turn over the Shanghai Jews. By this time, perhaps twenty thousand of them had taken refuge from Nazi Europe. Most settled first in the Hongkou district, in crowded dormitories and transitional apartments, then managed to find work and move to their own apartments elsewhere in the city. The Japanese, however, refused to bow to Nazi pressure to hand over the Jews, and instead confined them in a restricted zone—back in Hongkou. On February 18, 1943, the Japanese issued an order giving all Jews who had arrived from Europe after 1937 three months to move themselves and their businesses to a mile-square area of Hongkou, known officially as the "Designated Area for Stateless Refugees"—and unofficially known as the Shanghai Ghetto.

Historian David Kranzler describes the irony for Jews who had traveled across the world from Europe to escape the Nazis, then worked their way out of the squalid conditions in Hongkou to their own apartments in other parts of the city, only to be returned to Hongkou. "Refugees who had overcome great obstacles and had found a means of livelihood and residence outside the 'designated area' were forced to leave their homes and businesses for a second time and to relocate in a crowded, squalid area of less than one square mile with its own population of an estimated hundred thousand Chinese and eight thousand refugees," he said. Japanese guards patrolled the area and kept it under strict curfew. Everyone needed a pass to enter or leave. Food was rationed, and hunger was widespread, particularly in the harsh winter of 1943. Yet, amazingly, a vibrant cultural life emerged, with Jewish schools, newspapers, cafes, sports teams, Yiddish and

German theaters, even cabarets. A spirit of camaraderie flourished in the midst of shared adversity. After the war, the Shanghai Jews dispersed around the world, but survivors still gather periodically for reunions.

My father was not relocated to Hongkou; once again, his French citizenship sheltered him. Just as his French passport spared him confinement in the detention centers with the British and American citizens, it saved him from relocation to the Shanghai Ghetto with the Jewish refugees from Nazi Europe. Jews who lived in France, of course, were subject to Nazi law and turned over to concentration camps, but French subjects in the Middle East, China, and Southeast Asia were spared. The Japanese government rejected the most extreme aspects of their German allies' anti-Jewish policies, apparently considering race more significant than religion.

"Of course, you can't help but think what would happen if the Germans and Japanese got together and said, 'Let's do to the Jews in Shanghai what we are doing in Europe,' but on the contrary, the Germans put a lot of pressure on the Japanese to surrender the Jews but they refused. The worst they did was set up the small region in Hongkou where they

On February 18, 1943, the Japanese issued an order giving all Jews who had arrived from Europe after 1937 three months to move themselves and their businesses to a mile-square area of Hongkou, shown here, known officially as the "Designated Area for Stateless Refugees."

"Life was hard
for the Jews in
Hongkou, but
remember that
everyone
experienced
hardship during
the war. If you
needed
something that
was not
available in the
country where
you were living,
you couldn't get
it." Mike took
this photo of
residents buying
produce from a
street vendor,
circa 1943.

confined the Jews that came from Europe to escape the Nazis. I used to see a lot of them around Shanghai. They needed permission to go out and work and come back, but they were not in concentration camps or forced labor. Life was hard for the Jews in Hongkou, but remember that everyone experienced hardship during the war, the Japanese included, since they could not trade with other countries. If you needed something that was not available in the country where you were living, you couldn't get it."

&

Each neighborhood in Shanghai had a civil defense force responsible for seeing that civilians were at home or in a Red Cross shelter during air raid drills or if combat ever occurred. When the sirens went off, anyone on the street would be directed to the nearest shelter. The only people allowed outside at these times were the Red Cross volunteers, and my father had been selected by his neighbors to be one of their leaders. When the warning alarms sounded, he put on his white armband with the red cross, got on his bicycle, and rode straight to his assigned area to direct people to the shelter. He and the other Red Cross leaders were trained to carry people on stretchers to hospitals if direct combat ever broke out in Shanghai.

Yet even with the Red Cross armband, he took care never to disobey orders from the Japanese. "I did not want to take a chance because of lack of communication," he said, recalling the instance when he came to a barricade and was told not to go farther and so stayed put, while another man who insisted that he had to go through was beaten by the Japanese soldiers.

"The Japanese were such that if you did not come into disagreement with them or have anything to do with them, you were better off," he said. "First of all, the language barrier was tremendous. Second, any foreigner—by which I mean any non-Asian—was viewed with trepidation as to whether he was a friend or foe. The best bet was not to be overly friendly, because there was always that doubt as to whether you were spying on them or whether you were legitimately being a friend."

⊂⊃

My father made good friends who helped make the war years less tedious, including several men from Aleppo whom he met in Shanghai. Before the war, Shanghai had numerous social clubs where people gathered to eat, dance, and socialize. Syrian and Lebanese men, both Jewish and Christian, used to meet at the Rose and Leaf Club, paying dues to cover rent, a manager, and a Chinese cook whom they taught to prepare a few Syrian dishes. The men played cards or dice, sometimes for large sums of money, Dad said, though he himself did not gamble. Once the Japanese interned the Americans and British, however, the club lost many of its patrons and was forced to close, but he and some of the other men would meet on the street outside the club in the middle of the day to exchange war news and talk.

Through these friends, he met a Russian woman named Helen Lubchenko, who became his girlfriend. Shanghai had

The only people allowed outside when the warning alarms sounded were the Red Cross volunteers, and my father had been selected by his neighbors to be one of their leaders.

a large community of Russians who had left during the Bolshevik Revolution. Some neighborhoods even housed so many Russian expatriates that nearly everyone in the groceries and other stores spoke Russian, even the Chinese employees. (Russians were never interned in Shanghai, since Russia did not declare war on Japan until just a few weeks before the war ended.) Helen was from a White Russian family that had opposed the Communists, and Dad ate many meals at her home, learning about their Russian Orthodox Church and customs. "It gave me a chance to learn Russian," he said, so he could speak to her father, who spoke no English. (This was his fifth language, after Arabic, French, Turkish, and English. "It really was not difficult," he said. By contrast, curiously, he barely learned the Chinese dialect spoken there during all his years in Shanghai, partly because of the difficulty of acquiring a tonal language but mostly because there was so little direct interaction between Chinese and foreigners.)

Dating a woman of a different nationality and religion indicates just how much had changed since my father left Syria. Just a few years before, his mother had not let him go to the party of a Jewish girl he knew only casually because she did not feel the girl would have been a suitable candidate for marriage. Now he had a girlfriend of a religion he had not even ever encountered in Syria. Yet, like so many other changes he had lived through by that time, Dad saw the relationship as just something that emerged from new circumstances. He and his friends—Syrian men of Jewish and Christian backgrounds—would go out together and introduce their friends to one another, in a life with much-more-fluid cultural boundaries than he had known at home. He even took Helen to a synagogue with him on the High Holy Days. Still, he said, he knew he would never marry her because of the difference in religion. His plans remained what they had been: to come to the United States and help his family leave Syria. The woman eventually married an American GI who came into Shanghai at the end of the war, to help liberate it from the Japanese.

> Dating a woman of a different nationality and religion indicates just how much had changed since my father left Syria.

"He took a liking to her," Dad recalled. "We knew our relationship was not going to lead to anything further." Dad
even attended her wedding in Shanghai. The couple settled
in Buffalo, New York.

☙

For the duration of the war, the only way to send mail out
of the country was through a form issued by the Red Cross,
which provided space for twenty-five words. It would be sent
by the Red Cross to Switzerland and then routed to Syria,
arriving in Aleppo about six months later. On the reverse,
the recipient had room for twenty-five words in reply. Return
delivery to Shanghai would take another six months, so by
the time the letter got back to the sender, the fifty-word correspondence would have been in transit a full year! With
these constraints, my father obviously exchanged only skeletal information with his family and home, making the four
years of Japanese occupation long and worrisome for them.

"I must admit that at times it felt that the war would never
end," he said, "and I wondered whether I would survive it.
There was trepidation, anxious moments of not knowing
how long it would go on. Would it be a year? Two? Six?
Seven? How long would the war last, and what would happen when it ended?"

He recalled how he had felt several years earlier when he
learned that war had broken out in Europe, when he was still
living in Aleppo and on vacation with friends in Lebanon.
Hearing that Germany had invaded Poland and that England
and France then had declared war against Germany, he remembered thinking, "Good—they'll finish Germany in a
short time, and it'll be all over. We knew about what the
Nazis were doing to the Jews, and here we were talking about
America, England, and France declaring war on Germany.
We thought they would win the war in no time flat. The
French had the Maginot Line; we thought nothing could
penetrate it. These were trenches and fortifications all along

> "I must admit that at times it felt that the war would never end," my dad said, "and I wondered whether I would survive it."

the border, which no tanks could cross. But that was between France and Germany. Germany took Holland and Belgium and came down where there were no fortifications. They went all around the Maginot Line.

"It was the same thing with Japan. We thought, here Japan went into the war against the United States; the Americans will finish them off in no time. No one ever thought the war in the Far East was going to last almost four years! But a year went by, and the Japanese were gaining. And we knew that the more they gained, the longer it would take to kick them out. That gave us a kind of depressing feeling. At the beginning of the war, the Japanese marched through all of Southeast Asia. They took everything from northern to southern China to the Philippines to Malaya to the Dutch East Indies. The only places they did not reach were Australia and New Zealand. Otherwise they had all the other small islands in the Pacific, Okinawa, and the Solomon Islands, and so on.

"When you're in Shanghai and you hear about fighting for an island that is three or four thousand miles to the east— and that's a *little* island, and how many little islands are there? If it's going take that long for each one, obviously it's going take a long, long time for the war to be over. So you begin to think of these things, and they make you uncomfortable."

☙

In the summer of 1945, the Japanese began digging trenches and foxholes in the streets of Shanghai. Everyone understood that if the Allies invaded Shanghai, there would be fighting in the trenches—street by street, house by house.

"We knew that if such a thing happened, nobody would be safe, no matter what their citizenship or national origin," Dad said. "Everybody would be exposed to the fighting. They would keep on bombing that area and shooting flame-throwers. It could go back and forth, and the Japanese might be in overpowering numbers."

Some years later, he found out that two friends from Syria

who had been in Japan before the war were on their way back to Syria when their boat made a stop in Manila. The Japanese declared war in the Philippines while they were there, leaving them stranded in Manila. "We don't know exactly what happened," my father said, "but there must have been some misunderstanding as to what they did, or what the Japanese thought they did, and the two of them were killed by the Japanese. So nobody could claim they were safe just because they had certain papers or a certain nationality or certain friends in the government. When there's street-to-street fighting, it's impossible to know what's going to happen."

In the end, fortunately, this did not come to pass in Shanghai. In August of 1945, Dad learned that America had dropped two atomic bombs on the Japanese cities of Hiroshima and Nagasaki. "We did not know what the atomic bomb was, of course, but we knew that there was a lot of destruction and tens of thousands of casualties in both of those cities. We knew that Japan was seeking to end the war, and the only thing holding it back was that they wanted to preserve

Celebration of end of the war outside the Park Hotel. Note the victory banner in the crowd.

Victory celebration on the Bund.

the emperorship of Japan. Rumors were circulating a great deal, and it took a while before it was decided that the emperor would remain as a figurehead. Then the Japanese surrendered unconditionally. By that time, they had laid down their arms and were waiting either to be taken prisoner or for the Americans to come and occupy the areas they had occupied." So many Japanese soldiers had believed their government's reports of unflagging military success that when they received orders to surrender, as Dad heard, many committed suicide in the field. Even those with some access to reliable news reports were surprised by the suddenness of the war's end.

"Jubilation was widespread that the war was over, that we were spared," Dad said. The actual end of occupation then rolled in gradually. With such large distances between the many islands and countries that Japan had conquered, the American liberating forces took about two weeks from the end of the war to reach Shanghai and take control from the Japanese. That gave my father time to regroup and consider how to pick up his life.

Exporting the Family

"Everything was sort of at a standstill," my father said, describing the weeks and months after the war ended, "because nobody knew exactly how things were going to work out. We were really taking it day by day. The intention was always that the trip to the Far East was only a temporary thing, a stepping stone to the United States."

As military priorities abated and soldiers began returning home, transportation and communication networks in Southeast Asia gradually converted back from wartime operations to peacetime ones. Throughout the war, the major world powers had used whatever planes, ships, and trains were available to ferry soldiers and supplies from one continent to another. But by early 1946, as these systems were restored to civilian purposes, my father could finally resume contact once again with his family in Aleppo with letters that did not take an entire year to send and receive. He got back in touch with his Uncle Joe in New York, who told my father to stay in China and resume buying and shipping goods as he had done before the war.

So Dad remained in the Far East for another year and a half, traveling extensively to interior China, the Philippines, Hong Kong, and Japan to purchase hand-embroidered linens, tablecloths, and pillowcases to send to the United States "I had some at home for

Dad remained in the Far East for another year and a half, traveling extensively to interior China, the Philippines, Hong Kong, and Japan to purchase hand-embroidered linens, pillowcases, and tablecloths such as the one below to send to the U.S.

Mike, second from left on a tea break with friends, traveled to the little village of Swatow after the war to buy hand-embroidered linens for export to the United States, circa 1945.

quite a while," he said, "beautiful hand-made table linens with hand-embroidered napkins, similar to what you can find now in stores but a lot more elaborate. They really were beautiful. And there was a good market for them."

☙

Once the war ended, nationalist spirit surged in Syria as it did in countless other colonies of the major European powers. France had recognized the country as an autonomous republic on January 1, 1944, after more than twenty years of occupation and numerous Syrian attempts to claim independence. It would be two years, though, until France withdrew the last of its troops, April 17, 1946—the date Syria recognizes as its Independence Day.

In Aleppo, just outside the family home, my father's brother Elie witnessed a frightening event in 1945 during the tense period between Syria's nominative independence and France's troop withdrawal.

"Our house was situated on a main thoroughfare," he wrote in his fascinating memoir, *Alien at Home: Divine In-*

tervention, published in 2011. "Public trams ran parallel to our house. A newly built Sunni mosque across the street from our house held prayers five times a day, seven days a week. One specific Friday afternoon, men went inside the mosque for *juma,* congregational Sabbath prayers. The imam of this mosque had a penchant for inciting his congregants.

"I was sitting with Saleh by the window in his room. We observed the men coming out of the mosque. Simultaneously, a tram pulled up at the stop by our house. A soldier in a French uniform stepped down from the vehicle. A gang of Muslims that just left the mosque lunged at the soldier, striking him on all sides. They punched him, pounded him, and stabbed him with knives until he was dead. Days later, I heard that the soldier was not French but a local Muslim working for the French army. No one ever was held responsible."

Elie reported that two French teachers from the Lycée were murdered in May, just before the end of the school year. The school closed its doors at the end of the academic year (and remained shut for half a century, finally reopening in 1996). "Every hinting of French was wiped out," Elie said. "French words were removed from street signs and store banners. All that was French in Syria was no more."

Concurrently with this crest of anti-European sentiment, anti-Jewish fervor swelled in anticipation of the creation of a Jewish state in Palestine. Jews who could manage to get out—and had somewhere to go—continued to leave Syria. My father's family was still caught in the middle. When Elie's French college in Aleppo closed just a year before his graduation, he went to Beirut, Lebanon, to finish his degree. All his life he had dreamed of becoming a doctor, a dream that came close to fruition when he was admitted to medical school in France. But in May of 1946, my grandfather presented Elie with an announcement all too reminiscent of the one he had made to my father and Saleh five years before.

"Elie, I'm not a rich man," he recalls his father telling him. "We have lived comfortably over the years, but I am not rich. I can't afford to pay for your medical school. I can't afford

Elie witnessed a frightening event just outside the family home during the tense period in 1945 between Syria's nominative independence and France's troop withdrawal.

to financially support you for the next six or eight years. You will join your brother Miro in Shanghai. We will begin to make arrangements right away. Once there, you will be on your own to make your own decisions and choose what is best for you, just as Miro is doing. I can do no more."

Elie understood his father's reasons, much as my father had, but giving up his dream of becoming a doctor did not come easily. "Medical school. My life as a doctor. My hopes and dreams snatched from me. Was I upset? Was I disappointed? Yes, I was. This decision would haunt my entire life."

Just thinking back raised some questions in his mind about his father's decisions, his priorities, his reasons for not getting the family out of Syria earlier. But he also recognized the imperative for his father to step up efforts to get the family out. It was his turn to be "exported."

☙

In the summer of 1946, Elie made plans to travel to Shanghai to work with my father and, if all went as hoped, go to America. But the process of getting passports and visas for other countries was growing progressively more complicated, involving bribes, delays, and more bribes. When Sal—who had always been restless with his slow recovery from tuberculosis —announced that he wanted to leave with his brother, Elie welcomed the decision, "strictly on a selfish basis. I wanted his company." A friend, Moise Dweck, who had heard of Elie's and Sal's plans asked to join them, and they became a trio. They wrote my father in Shanghai, telling him their decision and asking his opinion of their business prospects. But Dad proved difficult to reach, since his work required frequent trips to Hong Kong, Manila, and other points in the Far East. In the meantime, they focused on getting passports and making travel arrangements across the world. "In my most vivid imagination, I could not have envisioned the bureaucratic complexities that confronted us," Elie wrote, describing weeks of questioning, bribes, delays, and referrals before the brothers got their passports.

In the summer of 1946, Elie made plans to travel to Shanghai to work with my father and, if all went as hoped, go to America.

Elie, at left, with Sal in Aleppo, prior to the start of their trip to Shanghai with a friend in 1946.

By that time, however, my father was making plans to leave Shanghai for America. He had seen business opportunities in China deteriorate, and was ready to make the move to America that had been halted by war five years earlier. He sent Elie the last news he wanted to hear: "Do not come to Shanghai. The future is bleak, at best. Business opportunities are meager."

But Elie and Saleh had already crossed a border in their minds. Nothing was going to dissuade them. "We had come so far," Elie said. "A few more difficulties would not deter us."

With air travel still new and communications emerging from a world at war, the trip had to be arranged piecemeal, arriving in one country before figuring out how to reach the next. Concerned about the aircraft's ability to stay aloft, travel agents would ask passengers' weight and advise them not to eat too much before boarding the plane!

"Adding to this, we failed to recognize our own immaturity and lack of experience," Elie said.

Their mother cried *"Allah ma'ak, Allah ma'ak"*—God be with you—over and over when Elie and Saleh left Syria on October 21, 1946.

"Thank you, Imee, for everything," Elie replied, using the Arabic pronunciation of the Hebrew word "ema" for mother. "I'll miss you, but let's not say goodbye. We'll see each other again. I know we will."

My grandfather accompanied Sal, Elie, and Moise on the train from Aleppo to Beirut, where they booked a flight to Cairo, but they could not get any information on flights from Cairo to Shanghai.

At the airport in Beirut, they said their goodbyes to their father. "Our goodbye stayed very vivid in my mind," Elie said. "Father was very stoic and strong. He spoke cheerfully and optimistically of our future. As I hugged him very warmly, I knew without any doubt in my heart that I was seeing him for the last time in my life."

> "As I hugged Father very warmly, I knew without any doubt in my heart that I was seeing him for the last time in my life," Elie said.

ᵒʒ

Only two airlines flew from Cairo to the Far East, Elie explained. Priority seating on those small planes went to diplomats and military personnel who had served in World War II, and civilians might not be assured of getting seats on the plane after refueling stops. The far-more-serious problem for Elie, Sal, and Moise, however, was religious. All the flights made a refueling stop at the Iraqi city of Basra, and Iraq required everyone who entered to have a transit visa *even if they did not get off the plane.* The Iraqi Consulate refused to issue them visas because their passports indicated that they were Jews.

Thus they were stranded for nearly two months in Cairo, chasing down any possibility, writing home for money to sustain them. One evening, leaving a restaurant where they had been socializing, a local man who knew their situation slipped them a piece of paper with the name of Kamal Tawfik, a

prominent Iraqi Jewish businessman who was staying at a hotel
in Cairo and might be able to help them. Tawfik, in fact,
agreed, without seeking payment for his aid, to ask his contacts
in the Iraqi government to help them get transit visas, which
they received in about two weeks. They were on their way.

Sal, second from
right, with
friends back in
Shanghai, 1947.

Even then, the grueling trip involved a long stay in Cal-
cutta, where flights to China were suspended for two weeks
pending investigation into two separate plane crashes on the
very route over the Himalayas that they planned to take.
While stranded there, Elie, who had never visited a dentist,
had a horrible toothache and received an emergency extrac-
tion! In addition, the travelers were clearly disquieted by the
two crashes when flights resumed, but they remained determined. After two refueling stops in China, they landed in
Shanghai at last on January 9, 1947.

 C3

The stepping stone that my grandfather had anticipated
for my father's passage from Syria to the United States had
become a six-year holding station. By December 1946, just

Dated December 4, 1946, this nonimmigrant visa application finally allowed my dad to leave Shanghai for the U.S., more than six years after arriving from Aleppo!

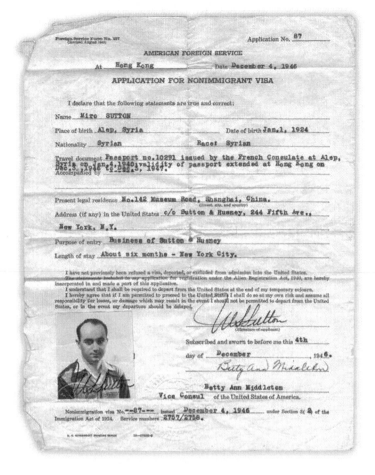

a few years before the Communist Revolution, Shanghai was no longer the cosmopolitan, international hub that my father had come to in February 1941. Recognizing the decline of economic opportunities in China, and the inadvisability of even a short visit to see his family in Aleppo, Dad wrapped up his affairs in Shanghai and arranged to come to the United States.

His first step was applying for a work visa at the American Consulate in Shanghai. He knew such a visa would let him stay for several months, figuring that he could show proof of employment once he was here and apply for an extension.

At the American Consulate, he found the huge waiting room so packed with people that "I said to myself, even if I stay the whole day, they might not call me, and I'll have to start all over again tomorrow. But I knew I was going to be in Hong Kong in a week or so on business. As soon as I got there, I went to the American Consulate and was sent into the office of the vice consul. She was a young woman whose name—I'll never forget it—was Betty Ann Middleton. I told her I would like a visa to go to the United States and presented some papers to satisfy her that I do business with my uncle. She looked at my papers and she said, 'I don't see why not.'

"At that time, the requirement if you were coming to the United States, even on a visit, was that you had to have an eye examination to see if you had glaucoma," he said. "So she made an appointment for me with an eye doctor, right on the same block as the consulate, and I went to see him and went back to her with the results the next day. She stamped my passport to come to the United States."

The visa was valid for departure anytime within twelve months. Dad completed his business in Hong Kong, went to the Philippines on a similar trip, and returned to Shanghai. He had only a six-month work visa but figured that would be enough time to settle up financially with his uncle and decide what to do next. His father's dream of relocating the family in the United States took a major step toward fulfillment.

When Elie and Saleh arrived in Shanghai in January, 1947, my father was in the Philippines on business.

CB

When Elie and Saleh arrived in Shanghai in January, 1947, my father was in the Philippines on a business trip. Bitterly disappointed not to be greeted by his brother, Elie and Sal moved into the YMCA and began to settle in. Sal took his brother to the Rose and Leaf Club, which had reopened after the war.

Sadly, however, Sal's time in Shanghai was again cut short by poor health. His health had been good on the trip, as Elie recalled, but perhaps the rigors of the journey and his reluctance to accept more stringent medical care had caught up with him. He had developed a severe cough, lost a great deal of weight and energy, and was spitting up blood. He soon wanted to return home to Syria.

"When I suggested to him that he should take better care of himself and that his condition did not have to be hopeless," my father recalled, "his reply was, 'When you guys think of the future, it's next year, or five or ten years. When I think of the future it's only for a much shorter time, so I am going to live it.'"

When Saleh returned to Aleppo that spring, after my father had left for the United States, the responsibility of notifying their family fell to Elie. "Saleh is coming home," Elie wrote their father. "His tuberculosis has returned and he is very sick. I hope he can survive the journey back to Aleppo." He did, but he died in late 1947 just a few months after returning to Aleppo.

Joe was twelve years old when his brother returned from Shanghai, weak and feverish. Their parents moved Saleh into a bedroom by himself, where their mother could care for him without the other children running in or out. Joe was hardly able to see his brother after that, but his earlier images stayed with him. "He was really a flamboyant man," Joe said adoringly. "He was very vibrant and very, very energetic, and he got hit hard."

My father did not learn of Saleh's death until sometime afterward. He had even sent a couple of letters to Saleh in Aleppo after his return but never got a reply. "Obviously they received the letters at home, and all they had to do was write back, but it is not customary of the Jewish community of Syria to mention that somebody died," he said, clearly still frustrated and saddened by the inability to experience a timely mourning for his brother.

"He had a no-care attitude," Dad said. "He took everything and made the best of everything. I was more serious. At times I wished I was more like he was, but being older, it was different. I made my choice, and he didn't have a chance to make his own choice."

> "[Saleh] had a no-care attitude," Dad said. "He took everything and made the best of everything. I was more serious."

Which Mike?
China Mike!

On April 30, 1947, my father sailed from Shanghai on the S.S. *General William H. Gordon,* a World War II Navy troop transport carrier that had been converted into a passenger ship. Arriving in San Francisco sixteen days later, he took a train to New Orleans, where his uncles Joe and Jack each had a retail store, although they lived in New York. Gazing out the train windows as he crossed the vast country, he marveled at America's open spaces and capacity to grow, such a dramatic contrast to the dense cities and villages of the Far East.

He spent a couple of weeks at the Roosevelt Hotel near the French Quarter. Jack had a store in the lobby, selling the same type of items my dad had exported from the Far East: hand-embroidered tablecloths, bed sheets, pillowcases, and handkerchiefs. Joe had a similar but larger store on Canal Street. While his uncles worked, he explored New Orleans, sightseeing and visiting with his cousins.

Since Syrian-Jewish custom calls for naming children after their grandparents, my father had several cousins named Mike, in honor of their paternal grandfather Meïr. This caused a bit of confusion one day in New Orleans.

At the house of his Uncle Joe's son, Mike, his Uncle Jack took a call from someone asking for Mike Sutton.

"Which one?" Jack replied.

At that moment, there were actually *three* Mike Suttons in the room: my father and two cousins, the oldest sons of

Postcard illustration showing the Roosevelt Hotel, New Orleans.

Joe and Jack! The shorter of these cousins was already known in the Syrian community as "Little Mike," and the other was "Big Mike." On the spot, Jack coined a nickname for my father: "China Mike." It stuck. Nicknames tend to endure in the Syrian-Jewish community, and Dad figured that if he had stayed in New York, he would have been known forever after as China Mike.

After his uncles completed what they needed to do in New Orleans, they took the train to New York with my father and his cousin Israel, the son of another brother, Abraham. In New York, Dad at last sat down with his Uncle Joe to settle up their financial matters. For the several years he had worked for his uncle, Dad paid his expenses from the business but asked that his wages be held back until he needed the money to get started on his own. He sat down with his uncle in Joe's office on Fifth Avenue and told him how much money he figured he was owed. His uncle wanted more time to look over the calculations, but my father could not afford to wait, since he was in the country on only a six-month work visa.

"I was on pins and needles all this time," he said, "because I had only a temporary visa, was not yet a citizen, and needed to settle financial matters before deciding what to do next with my life." It took a few months to agree to a compromise, which came only after my father had hired an attorney. By then Dad had moved out of Joe's house in Brooklyn and moved in with his cousin, Rachel Haber, and her husband, Raymond, with whom he started a business importing hand-embroidered linens and baby clothes.

CB

To an outsider, a walk down Brooklyn's Ocean Parkway in 1947 must indeed have felt like being transported to "Aleppo in Flatbush," to borrow the charming subtitle of one of Syrian writer Joseph A.D. Sutton's books. Syrian groceries sold Middle Eastern foods and spices, women boiled pots of

> On the spot, Jack coined a nickname for my father: "China Mike." It stuck.

rice and *hamud* for Friday night dinners, men played *toleh* with friends after work while chatting in Arabic.

But to the Syrian immigrants themselves, America had a very different ambiance. By then, the Syrian community in Brooklyn had reached tens of thousands spread over a large geographical area, not self-contained as it had been in Aleppo. In the New York melting pot, Syrian Jews found themselves a minority even among Jews. The far-more-numerous Ashkenazi Jews from Europe and Russia, far more assimilated into American culture, spoke disparagingly of these "Arab Jews" who lived so differently; some even doubted that these Arabic-speaking immigrants were really even Jewish. The community remained as tight-knit as in Syria, but it floated within a huge American city far different from the provincial town they had left. Dad knew some Syrians who found American ways so alienating that they quickly left and moved to Palestine.

Yet perhaps for having lived on his own in Shanghai for six years, my father found his adjustment to America easier than that of many who came directly from Aleppo. For one thing, he arrived fluent in English and familiar with American expressions and customs (from all those American movies!). Those years of living alone and fending for himself had heightened his sense of resourcefulness and adaptability—as well as his sense of independence—a mixed blessing while trying to settle back into the Syrian Jews' communal lifestyle.

One of his most difficult adjustments was to the American pace of life. When his uncle was still in Shanghai, they would shut the office for a leisurely lunch at noon, have afternoon tea at a nearby hotel, and close up for the day by five. He developed a similar routine working on his own in Shanghai after the war. On business trips to Hong Kong, he and his friends would take the Star Ferry at 9:30 in the morning from the Peninsula Hotel in Kowloon to the office they shared in downtown Hong Kong, break for lunch together at noon, have afternoon tea at a nearby hotel, and end the

In the New York melting pot, Syrian Jews found themselves a minority even among Jews.

workday soon after. Once he started working with Raymond Haber in New York, he traveled an hour by subway from Brooklyn to Manhattan, worked all day with just a half-hour lunch break—and before long had dropped twenty pounds!

☃

In November 1947, the United Nations issued its "Partition Plan for Palestine," calling for a complicated division into a separate Jewish state and the Arab state of Palestine. Arabs throughout the Middle East and North Africa went on rampages in protest. With historical perspective, many observers now conclude that these were not spontaneous eruptions of rage but rather mass insurgencies orchestrated by the Arab governments and police forces.

Mobs estimated at up to a hundred thousand people stormed Aleppo's Jewish quarter for days, breaking windows and destroying Jewish-owned businesses and homes. My grandparents hid in the basement with their children Margo, Ralph, Joe, Morris, and Edgar. When they heard a crowd of rioters break into the house, they snuck out and ran to the Armenian neighborhood, where a Christian man whom my grandfather knew through business gave them refuge for a few days until the hostilities ebbed.

My father's brother Joe, who was twelve years old at the time, told me: "When they divided Palestine to grant the State of Israel, Arabs in Syria revolted against those decisions and against the Jews. They went to every *shul,* every place they knew of as a Jewish congregation, and they took everything out of it and burned it—the Torahs, the prayer books, everything. Our house was in the center of town, and it was one of the only family houses that were burned. We were the only people [in the neighborhood] that had a one-family house, and it was very well known that it was a Jewish family that owned it. As long as they were burning everything, they went into the house, took the drapes, dipped them in gasoline, and burned them."

One of the most difficult adjustments my dad had to make was to the American pace of life. He worked all day with just a half-hour lunch break—and before long had dropped twenty pounds!

Mobs estimated of several thousand people stormed Aleppo's Jewish quarter, breaking windows and destroying Jewish-owned businesses and homes and chanting anti-Jewish slogans. My grandparents hid in the basement with their children Margo, Ralph, Joe, Morris, and Edgar. When they heard a crowd of rioters break into the house, they snuck out and ran to the Armenian neighborhood, where a Christian man whom my grandfather knew through business gave them refuge for a few days until they felt safe to return home.

No Jews in Aleppo were killed in the riots (despite rumors to the contrary), but more than two hundred Jewish homes, shops, and schools, an orphanage, a youth club, and all 18 of the city's synagogues incurred serious damage—including my grandparents' neighborhood synagogue and the adjoining school that my father had attended and where his younger siblings now studied.

My father, living in New York by this time but on a business trip to the Philippines, learned of these events through a telegram from his father. "It did not surprise me," he said, knowing of the escalating conflict between Jews and Arabs in the Middle East, but he was frightened about the implications

The family home, shown here when my Uncle Joe visited it in 2000, was left temporarily uninhabitable by the rampage, needing five or six months of repairs. Joe reported that the house was "exactly as we left it."

With my father
in New York and
Elie in China,
much of the
responsibility for
the family
business and
long-term
planning shifted
to the next son,
Ralph, shown at
right here with a
friend in Aleppo,
circa 1948.

for his family: "My concern was for their safety." He was saddened and haunted by the image of his parents, sister, and
younger brothers sneaking out a basement door, running from
their home in fear. Just a few years before, he had been in
school in Aleppo with Muslims, Christians, and Jews studying
amicably together. Fortunately his father was friendly enough
with the Armenian who took the risk of sheltering seven Jews
in his home. Dad speculated that even some of his father's
Muslim contacts wanted to help them—though not enough
to overcome fear of consequences from the Syrian government.

With my father in New York and Elie in China, much of
the responsibility for the business and long-term plans shifted
to the middle sons, Ralph and Joe, just fifteen and twelve
years old, respectively. My grandfather continued going to his
office and running his business, with a clearer understanding
than ever that he must find a way for the family to leave.

CS

In New York, my father continued his partnership with Raymond Haber, the husband of his cousin Rachel, importing hand-embroidered textiles from the Far East. By this time, Elie had set up an office in Shanghai, and he filled many of their orders. Dad returned to the Far East himself in the winter of 1947 and again in the spring of 1948, traveling to Hong Kong, the Philippines, and Swatow to commission orders for hand-embroidered linens, infant dresses, and nightgowns.

This time, he crossed the Pacific by plane: the glamorous Pan American Clipper.

The Clipper boasted "Sleeperettes," seats that reclined until they were almost flat so that passengers could—or so the advertising claimed—"slip into a restful, unbroken night's slumber." In reality, the noise and vibrations of the propeller-driven plane were so intense that Dad hardly slept a wink on the forty-hour flight from Manila to San Francisco, with several refueling stops along the way. After checking in to a hotel in San Francisco late in the evening, he took a bath and went to sleep to rest up for the next day's flight to New York. When he awoke, he called the hotel operator to ask what time it was. "She said seven in the evening! I had slept through the whole day. So I stayed in San Francisco for a couple of days and then flew back to New York."

On May 14, 1948, the British Mandate of Palestine ended, and British military forces left. That day, Israeli leader David Ben-Gurion declared the creation of the State of Israel.

CS

On May 14, 1948, the British Mandate of Palestine ended, and British military forces left. That day, Israeli leader David Ben-Gurion declared the creation of the State of Israel. Just a day later, a coalition of Egypt, Jordan, Syria, Lebanon, and Iraq—joined by contingents from Saudi Arabia and Yemen and Palestinian militia—declared war on the new country.

"The Arabs thought they would win in less than the twinkling of an eye, and that it would take no more than a day or two from the time the Arab armies crossed the border until all the colonies were conquered and the enemy would throw down his arms and cast himself on their mercy," wrote Palestinian journalist and historian Aref el-Aref.

By May 14, many Arab residents of what was now Israel had already left or been driven from their homes. In the months of sniper attacks, bombings, and riots before the British pullout, first the wealthiest Palestinians and then the poorer ones fled for neighboring Arab countries or the homes of friends in smaller Palestinian towns to escape the crossfire. As the Arab armies entered on May 15, hundreds of thousands more Palestinians left for outlying regions or neighboring countries, anticipating a quick Arab victory followed by a return to their homes. Crowds of Palestinians lined the roads to cheer the advancing Arab armies, confident the conflict would soon end.

What is far less well known is that even greater numbers of Jews fled or were expelled from Muslim countries after the creation of Israel.

But the Israelis, having amassed an arsenal since World War II and drafted a large number of men and women, stopped the advancing armies. They ultimately pushed back the Arab forces and emerged with much more land than they had been granted in the 1947 Partition Plan which the Arab countries had rejected. Egypt signed a truce with Israel on February 24, 1949, and the other Arab countries followed.

Estimates of how many Arab residents of Palestine left their homes before and during the war vary widely, but it is safe to conclude that from 1947 to 1949, more than six hundred fifty thousand became refugees. Some returned to their homes after the war; others were absorbed into neighboring Arab countries. Still others remained in refugee camps, where many of their descendants live in precarious conditions to this day.

What is far less well known is that even greater numbers of Jews fled or were expelled from Muslim countries after the creation of Israel. Over eight hundred thousand Jews left Morocco, Algeria, Tunisia, Libya, Egypt, Lebanon, Syria, Iraq,

Yemen, and Aden from 1948 to the early 1970s as a result of backlash against the creation of Israel.

Jews whose families had lived in these regions for centuries side by side with Christians and Muslims found themselves prisoners in their own countries, escaping by way of smugglers, bribes, and disguises. Many of them left with no more than what they could carry, leaving behind property that was confiscated by the government or the people who moved into their homes. They have relocated to and integrated themselves into Israel, Europe, and North and South America, defining themselves not as refugees of Arab countries but as citizens of their new ones. Jewish communities in the Middle East and North Africa, where the ancestors of those who fled had lived for thousands of years, have vanished.

The pages of his passport track Dad's return to the Far East in the winter of 1947 and again in the spring of 1948, traveling to Hong Kong, the Philippines, and Swatow to commission orders for hand-embroidered linens, infant dresses, and nightgowns.

ℂℋ

The Syrian government retaliated against the establishment of the Jewish state with severe restrictions on the rights of Jews. They were barred from leaving the country and were not issued passports or drivers' licenses. They were not allowed to sell their property. Jewish businesses were boycotted, and Arabs were absolved from obligation to repay debts to Jews.

"If you were a Jew, you could not travel, you could not have a passport, you could not sell your property," Joe told me. "They burned the school that we were attending [the Jewish school affiliated with their synagogue], and now we had to find a different school that would accept us. We weren't able to sell the house. Muslims did not have to repay debts to the Jews—because the Israelis did not pay their debts to the refugees that left Palestine at that time; that was the explanation that was given to us."

My grandfather still had a plan in place, but time worked against him. He had no choice but to continue the business in order to save money to get the rest of the family out, but it became harder and harder to collect on the products he sold. Always a self-sufficient, fiercely independent man, committed to working for himself rather than in partnership with his brothers, he found himself increasingly helpless. His clients used to come to his office to pay him; now he went to his Muslim customers for collection of debts that they were suddenly not obliged to repay. Joe recalls skipping school to go with his father on dangerous excursions to collect money, watching his father beg for money he had earned.

"Nothing was done in cash," Joe explained. "Everything was in promissory notes. At that time, believe it or not, nobody had any money in the bank. Most of my father's assets were in credits that were owed to him that people never acknowledged or paid."

The Syrian government's refusal to allow Jews to leave—a policy that at first seems incomprehensible toward a people

"If you were a Jew, you could not travel, you could not have a passport, you could not sell your property," my Uncle Joe told me.

they suddenly considered their enemy—reflected shrewd economic, political, and military strategy. Retaining Jews within Syria would keep them from helping to develop the new country of Israel just across the border and serving in its army. Maintaining Jewish communities in Syria's major cities would also act as a hedge against Israeli military attacks and thwart efforts to grow the Israeli economy. Jews may also have been deemed necessary to the Syrian economy, since they ran so many businesses. Whatever the reasons, Jews who had been accepted, welcomed members of Syrian society were suddenly required to get authorization for even short trips out of the country, and even then, they had to leave family members behind as collateral to ensure their return. The country's Jewish population of thirty thousand in 1948 began leaving in droves through underground channels.

CB

No longer able to return to Syria, my father committed himself in 1948 to making a life in America, and set out on the long, winding road toward citizenship rather than continuing to apply for visa extensions every six months. In the meantime, he went to the Syrian Consulate in New York to renew his passport, since the one he had expired.

"I walked into the consul's office, in the Empire State Building," he said, "and I looked at him and he looked at me—we were in the same class together in the Mission Laïque! So we spent a good half-hour chatting. He was Muslim. In effect, what he told me was that he could not extend it but he would take the passport and send it to Syria so that the Syrian government could send me a new one. I knew if I gave it to him, I would never receive a new one back. I knew if I wasn't Jewish, it wouldn't have been required; I think it was established that if it was a Jew [applying for a passport], you don't extend it."

Without a valid passport, he could not extend his work visa, and as a Jew, he could not renew his Syrian passport or return home. In a nutshell, he was stateless.

No longer able to return to Syria, my father committed himself in 1948 to making a life in America, and set out on the long, winding road toward citizenship.

"So I went to the immigration office and filled out an application for permanent residency status, citing persecution if I were to return to Syria. I had the telegram in my pocket that I received from my father a few months earlier while I was in the Far East, which stated that our house in Aleppo was set on fire by the Arabs, who went on a rampage of burning, looting, and killing upon hearing of the United Nations' vote on the State of Israel. I had decided to hold on to this, knowing that it might help in getting my request approved, since I could no longer return home to Syria.

Getting married to an American citizen would automatically make Dad eligible for legal residency and eventual citizenship.

"Some two or three months went by until I heard from the immigration office advising me, 'We do not think that you qualify to be given Legal Resident Status.' However, the letter went on to state, 'If you would like, we will send your application to Washington for their review and final approval or denial.' I replied, 'Though I think the decision of the New York Immigration Office is unjust, I would like my application to be forwarded to Washington for review.' I knew that once it was sent to Washington, it would be at best two or three years, if not longer, before I would hear from them. Meanwhile, getting married to an American citizen would automatically make me eligible for legal residency and eventual citizenship"—although he had no particular future wife in mind at the time.

☙

The urgency that Syrian Jewish families felt, whether in Aleppo or Brooklyn, to find suitable husbands for their daughters recalls scenes from Jane Austen or "Downton Abbey." By the time a woman reached twenty, she would face intense pressure to marry and start a family. My father had arrived in New York's Syrian Jewish community as a handsome bachelor in his twenties, amid many young women looking for a husband. His fresh face soon became very popular in the community.

Men had a little more time to work with in finding a

mate. A Syrian man might not tie the knot until he was in his late twenties or even early thirties and gainfully employed. Women married young—not necessarily as young as my grandmother and her contemporaries, who were having babies by their early teens—but time was a harsh taskmaster. If a man and woman dated even a couple of times, there would be "talk": What were the man's intentions? Was he going to propose? My father was even lobbied by relatives of women he had barely met. Out of the blue one day, he received a phone call from the uncle of a young woman named Sarah, whom he had seen around the community but never dated. "I never knew the guy from Adam! He came to the city and took me out to lunch, and he started to talk about Sarah. I said 'I really don't know; we never went out.' To appease him, I said I'd take her out. But I never did," Dad said.

"That's how it was in the community," he explained. "If you take someone out more than once, you keep it on the QT. This was especially for the girl's sake. If someone dated her several times but did not propose, the word would get around that, 'She wasn't good enough for so and so.'"

In 1949 the communists took control of Shanghai. Practically overnight, Elie said, the old Chinese flags came down and Communist flags went up.

☙

Elie was living in Shanghai through the Communist takeover in 1949. Initially lonely and uneasy about being so far from his family, he came to enjoy the fast-paced, glamorous life of international commerce and nightclubs bustling with people from all over the world. When he first arrived, the Maoists were gaining power in Manchuria, in far-northern China, but Shanghai seemed far from these developments. With World War II over and commerce once again in full swing, it seemed inconceivable that Mao and his army would soon march south and overthrow the ruling Kuomintang government.

Elie told me he feared this takeover as it approached, but when it finally happened, he was surprised by how easily the Communists took control and forced the Kuomintang to the island of Formosa. Practically overnight, he said, the old Chinese flags came down and Communist flags went up. Posters of Mao suddenly were everywhere. Elie was able to continue running the exporting business with America for a while because the Communists initially did not shut down trade. But when China entered the war against the United States in Korea, commerce between the two countries ceased, and Elie acted on his plans to come to the United States.

Unable to renew his expired Syrian passport in Shanghai, Elie found himself stateless, just as my father had been. From New York, my father inquired into obtaining a permit for Elie to enter Japan for the ostensible purpose of promoting the Chinese goods that Elie exported, with hopes that Elie could obtain a work visa in Tokyo to come to the United States. In early 1950, he received a little form that my father had forwarded from the State Department in Washington, a permit issued by General Douglas MacArthur giving Elie permission to enter Japan.

"To me, Mike had pulled off a miracle," Elie wrote. "Little did I realize that the permit was issued under the presumption that I was an American businessman, not a stateless foreigner living and doing business in Communist China."

Needing permission from the authorities in Shanghai to travel to Japan, Elie applied for and received an exit visa to promote his Chinese products—but he let the visa expire, reluctant to leave his Shanghai lifestyle. But with America and China at war in Korea, Elie became convinced he had to leave Shanghai for Japan. There he obtained a work visa to the United States, arriving in October of 1950.

"To me, Mike had pulled off a miracle," Elie wrote.

ɞ

At one of the large parties that were common in the Syrian community, my father met a lovely young woman named Cynthia Beyda. Cynthia had grown up in a Syrian Jewish family in Arlington, Virginia, just outside Washington, D.C. As a child, she had visited her cousins in Brooklyn frequently

Cynthia Beyda, left, on the porch of her Arlington, Virginia, home with her mother, Esther. When my mother reached her early twenties, her parents rented an apartment in New York so she could find a Syrian husband, circa 1949.

on family trips, keeping ties to the Syrian community. When she was in her early twenties, her parents rented an apartment in Manhattan at the Franconia Hotel on West 72nd Street, just off Central Park on the Upper West Side, so their daughter could find a Syrian husband. (In the Syrian community, even a match between a Sephardic and an Ashkenazi Jew was and still is considered "intermarriage.")

Cynthia found Manhattan exciting and cosmopolitan compared with Washington, which she remembers as a "little hick town" at the time. Moving to the city also meant having a ready-made set of friends, since she had always been close with her New York cousins. She loved being among the large, embracing community, a welcome contrast to Arlington, where she and her brothers had been the only Jewish children in school and occasional targets of anti-Semitic slurs. She would drive the family car out to Brooklyn from the Franconia for holidays and parties, and have her cousins and friends to the apartment.

"I had not been in New York too long before I met Cynthia Beyda," my father recalled (with much the same matter-of-fact tone he used in relating political events). "In the Syrian community, they used to have lots of dances and parties in people's home, with maybe twenty or thirty people, and I met her there once or twice. Sometimes she would have a party herself. I decided, after being invited to a couple of her parties, that I should take her out. So I called up and I made a date to take her out, and I guess we hit it off. So we continued dating. One day, after we were going out maybe two or three times, I was invited by her mother and father to go out to dinner, and I got in the car and they locked the doors."

"Come on," I interrupted. "Is this a true story?"

"Not exactly. They didn't lock the doors. But they questioned me as to what my intentions were. So I said, 'I think we're serious with one another,' and we left it at that. I don't blame them. In the community, if you're going out with someone, the whole community knows about it, so you don't do it for an extended period of time without making your intentions known."

"So let me get this straight. You were calling her as, just, reciprocation for inviting—"

"Well, not just reciprocation. You don't just call up for reciprocation. You call because you like the individual and you want to know more about them—come on, that's a loaded question."

"Of course it is! But I'm curious—what was it like? Did you know she was the one from the beginning, or did it kind of take you by surprise? You know, everybody wonders that about their parents."

I asked my dad, "Did you know [Mom] was the one from the beginning, or did it kind of take you by surprise?"

In the end, good judgment prevailed. Cynthia Beyda and Mike Sutton were married at the East Midwood Jewish Center in Brooklyn on November 5, 1950.

"Well, ask her. I think she'll probably . . ."

"I'm not asking her. I'm asking you!"

"Like I said, usually girls have more recollections about such details than men do."

Mom *does* remember the phone call from a young Mike Sutton inviting her out on a date. She nearly refused because she had the impression that her cousin Paulette had a crush on him. Mom had noticed the handsome young man walking down the street with a friend shortly after he arrived; word about new, single arrivals from Syria (even by way of China) spread through the community like wildfire. She was about to turn him down out of loyalty to her cousin, but her good friend Sally Bijou, who was visiting my mother that evening, urged her to accept.

After the wedding, my grandparents —the business completed of marrying off their daughter to a suitable Syrian husband —returned to Washington, D.C.

In the end, good judgment prevailed. Cynthia Beyda and Mike Sutton were married at the East Midwood Jewish Center in Brooklyn on November 5, 1950, and honeymooned at the Pierre Hotel in Manhattan. My father's immediate family was still in the Middle East with the exception of his brother Elie, who had arrived from Shanghai just two weeks before and served as best man. My mother's family from Washington of course attended, along with their many New York relatives. After the wedding, my parents moved into the apartment that my grandparents had rented at the Franconia Hotel in Manhattan, and my grandparents—the business completed of marrying off their daughter to a suitable Syrian husband—moved back to Washington, D.C.

Crossings

ot long after my parents married, Mom went down to Washington for a short trip to see her parents. She came down with the flu and had to stay a few extra days, so my father went down on the weekend to see her. While he was there, he got a phone call from his Uncle Jack in New Orleans.

The manager of Jack's store in New Orleans had wanted to open a store of his own in Houston and had signed an agreement for a building there. Not wanting to lose a good manager, Jack offered him a better arrangement and persuaded him to stay at the New Orleans store, but he wanted someone to take over the Houston lease to get his manager out of his obligation and remove his incentive to leave.

Dad was already scouting around for a new opportunity. American engagement in the Korean War in mid-1950 led to a trade embargo between America and China, once again bringing his importing business to a halt. He explored new business opportunities, perhaps importing from Europe. Accepting Jack's offer would mean he and my mother would need to move to Texas right away. He discussed the decision with his brother Elie, who had moved into the room my father rented in Brooklyn before he and my mother married. Elie and Dad had been exploring ways of going into business together.

I can hardly imagine my grandparents' reaction to the idea of their only daughter moving to Houston. New York was about four hours away from them by train or car, but it was familiar. It was where my grandparents had married and started their family, and where they still often visited relatives. But

Dad was already scouting around for a new opportunity. American engagement in the Korean War in mid-1950 led to a trade embargo between America and China, once again bringing his importing business to a halt.

Texas? Halfway across the country, with no Syrian community? It might as well have been Mars. So my grandfather approached his son-in-law with an alternate—and perhaps not entirely ingenuous—plan: move to Washington and take over his retail store. He said he wanted to retire from the successful Beyda's Children's Apparel, at F and Twelfth Streets in the heart of the city's downtown shopping district, and was ready to pass it on.

My parents weighed the options carefully. "I knew Abe Beyda did well in Washington," Dad said, "so if he was thinking of retiring, I thought that would be a good chance for me to get into the retail business." The downside would be leaving Brooklyn, where his brother Elie had recently arrived and the family still in the Middle East hoped to settle soon. My parents had been considering moving from the Franconia Hotel in Manhattan to a house in the Brooklyn Syrian community. Relocating to Houston initially would take them far from New York, but Dad figured the move would not be permanent. After a few years working in Texas with his brother Elie, he assumed, they would return to Brooklyn and rejoin the Syrian community.

My mother's parents lobbied hard for Washington. Elie, recognizing that my father had lived alone for nearly ten years and that the rest of their surviving family was still in the Middle East, encouraged his brother to find a place among my mother's family. Mom realized that it would be easier to start a life in Washington now that Dad's business with China had ceased. And though she loved living in New York, near her friends and cousins, she didn't want to disappoint her parents.

The options would take my parents in starkly different directions: Would their children grow up among the Syrian community in Brooklyn, knowing the proper time to wait after eating meat before having a glass of milk, attending a synagogue where women and men sat separately, and not turning lights on or off on the Sabbath? Would they grow up in Maryland, close to my maternal grandparents and cousins, going to public school and having friends of other religions? Or might we have been raised in Houston—the hardest of the three paths to imagine!

> My parents weighed the options carefully. "I knew Abe Beyda did well in Washington," Dad said, "so if he was thinking of retiring, I thought that would be a good chance for me to get into the retail business."

In the end, they chose Washington. But my grandfather did not retire from the business at that point as he had said he would, and instead stayed on, working with my father as well as his sons, Joe and Irving Beyda, and my mother's uncle, Daniel Beyda. This arrangement was not what had led my father to move to Washington, and caused him a great deal of frustration. Five years later, my grandfather did retire, and Dad took over the store. By then most of the other family members had gone off on their own. Irving was running another children's clothing store that my grandfather had opened in the Friendship Heights area of Maryland. Joe had opened a women's clothing store on Connecticut Avenue. Danny Beyda continued operating his women's clothing business on the ground floor of what was now my father's store for a year or two, and later opened his own store on Fourteenth Street. In time, my father opened three other stores in the Washington suburbs, where he and my mother raised three children and have lived ever since.

And so it came to pass that my siblings and I grew up in Maryland in our little "satellite" of Brooklyn's Syrian community, much more culturally Americanized and religiously assimilated than our New York cousins. But I wonder if the seeds of that decision had not actually been sown many years before. By the time my father left New York, he had lived away from his family for ten years. As much as he looked forward to the arrival of his brothers and mother, he had lost some comfort with the clannishness of the Syrian community after living alone for so long. Perhaps he had inherited the independent streak of his own father, who had chosen to work for himself in Aleppo rather than come to America and work with his brothers. For her part, my mother had already spent her life outside the community, seeing her Brooklyn cousins only on vacations, since her parents moved from Brooklyn to Washington shortly after they married. Individual history and personalities converged with economic factors to lead this portion of the family to settle away from the larger Syrian-Jewish community. From my vantage point on

In time, my father opened three other stores in the Washington suburbs, where he and my mother raised three children and have lived ever since.

the margins of that community, it seems that the inclination to identify with a group rather than as an individual requires immersion, continuity, an unbroken chain. Multigenerational events and choices appear to have weakened those links long before my parents chose Washington over Texas.

❦

Back in Aleppo my grandfather's health had taken a turn for the worse. In late 1949 he went to a doctor because of increasingly severe headaches and diminishing vision.

In Aleppo, my father's family moved back into their home about six months after the riots, but life did not return to normal. Tension between Muslims and Jews was increasing, and my grandfather's health had taken a turn for the worse. In late 1949 he went to a doctor—something one did only in extreme circumstances—because of increasingly severe headaches and diminishing vision. The doctor diagnosed the early stages of a brain tumor. Medical options were rudimentary in Aleppo, so the doctor suggested my grandfather go to Beirut for treatment not available in Syria.

This would have been easy just two years before. But after the establishment of Israel in May 1948, although trains and buses continued to pass from Syria to Lebanon, the Syrian government forbade Jews to leave the country except in rare circumstances. Jews might be granted temporary travel permits for medical emergencies—but only with payment of a substantial sum to be reimbursed when the travelers returned, and only if some family members stayed behind in Syria.

So the family had to choose who would accompany my grandparents and who would stay behind. Joe, fifteen years old, was chosen to escort his father and mother. He filed an application for a temporary medical visa, which was granted only after my grandfather submitted a letter from the doctor and paid a deposit of $500 for each of the three travelers. Ralph, three years older than Joe, would stay behind in Aleppo with Margo, Morris, and Edgar, looked after by their mother's sisters, Latife and Eugenie. As the oldest son at home, Ralph, at eighteen, became the man of the household.

"When I went to Beirut," Joe said, "I didn't think 'I'm not coming back.' We were facing the events that were happening at the time. I felt that I was leaving to help Dad get better, and I would do what I needed to do for the business. It was not with the intention of not coming back. Life wasn't life-threatening [in Syria]. Perhaps we would even return to Syria and continue the business, if we could."

Safely relocated in Beirut for medical treatment, my grandfather began receiving radiation for his tumor. In Aleppo, Ralph had the responsibility to do what he could with his father's business and try to collect money owed to it, while figuring out ways to get Margo, Morris, Edgar, and himself to Lebanon.

The prohibition against Jewish emigration from Syria posed no small obstacle. Jews who were caught trying to leave faced the death penalty or prison with hard labor. Thousands left through clandestine channels nonetheless, trafficked out individually or in small groups by hired smugglers to escape the escalating oppression.

From left, Margo, Joe, Edgar, Morris, and Ralph in Aleppo, 1946.

"There were people who knew how to do it," Joe explained, "because the restriction [against emigration] was only on Jews. They camouflaged you [as an Arab] and put you on a train or bus from Aleppo to Beirut, and you got away." Margo, Ralph, Morris, and Edgar would cross the border to Lebanon one by one with the assistance of these smugglers after my grandparents and Joe left Aleppo.

But after several months of treatment at the American University Hospital in Beirut, my grandfather's doctor saw no improvement and suggested that he go to Israel for better options.

There was just one problem: Lebanon did not recognize the new country of Israel and would not let anyone across the border. But as Joe explained, "The relationship between Israel and Lebanon was not *openly* good, but it was *undercover* good." Word circulated among Jews that they could board a ship at night in Beirut and be received in the morning by officials at the Israeli coast. (Israeli officials would not have let Muslims enter this way, Joe explained, but Jews were welcomed to build up the new country.)

Margo was the first of the siblings to be smuggled from Syria to Lebanon. My grandfather had decided to take her with him to Israel in hopes of finding a surgeon who could correct her elephantiasis. Joe would accompany them.

And so first Margo and my grandfather, then Joe a few weeks later, went by boat in the middle of the night from Lebanon to Israel in 1952, leaving my grandmother alone in Beirut living for a short time in a *pension* with friendly neighbors. My grandfather checked into the hospital in Tel Aviv that his doctor in Beirut had recommended. Margo had surgery at the same hospital to attempt to correct her elephantiasis, but the operation was not successful and she continued to walk with a limp. After getting out of the hospital, she moved in with a sister of her mother's named Milo, and Joe moved in with Ramiza, another sister living in Israel.

Ralph was the last to leave Aleppo, in 1952, after Joe, Margo, and their father had already gone to Israel. He had liquidated what remained of his father's inventory and col-

There was just one problem: Lebanon did not recognize the new country of Israel and would not let anyone across the border.

My grandmother, with her youngest sons (from left) Edgar, Joe and Morris, on the balcony of the apartment where they lived between fleeing Aleppo and coming to the United States, circa 1956.

lected what he could of money they were owned. Prohibited from selling the family home, he rented it to a Muslim sheikh, collecting three years' rent in advance.

Ralph recounted his passage across the border from Syria into Lebanon alone, camouflaged in Arab clothing. He had paid a train conductor to take him to Tripoli disguised as his son. If the border authorities asked questions, the conductor was ready to say, "This is my son; he gets good marks and wants to go to a better school in Lebanon, so I am taking him to Beirut." He had urged Ralph to pretend to be asleep if this happened and let him answer all the questions, since Ralph's accent would give him away as Jewish. Sure enough, when the ticket inspector came through at 2 a.m., Ralph heard the conductor say, "He's my son. He's asleep." He closed his eyes as tightly as he could until he heard the conductor pass. In Tripoli he de-boarded the train and caught a bus to Beirut.

"God does things for a reason," my late Aunt Sondra said, hearing her husband Ralph describe the journey. "Me, I'm scared at my own shadow. He traveled out of the country as a child."

CB

Despite receiving some of the best treatments available
when they arrived in Israel in 1952, my grandfather's health
did not improve.

"We tried everything possible," Joe recalled. "It didn't work.
He didn't get any better. He started deteriorating more and
more. He couldn't remember me, and he couldn't remember
who he was." Joe moved his father from the hospital to a nursing home, where he took a job to help defray the costs.

Later Joe and Margo had to move their father to a gov-
ernment-subsidized home farther from where they lived. Joe
would visit as often as he could, every couple of weeks, but
he was not there when his father died in August of 1953.

This father of eight children, so beloved, respected, and
admired within his community, died alone, with none of his
family or loved ones around him, and was buried in a cemetery outside Tel Aviv.

With no mail service between Israel and Lebanon, Joe could
not notify his mother directly of her husband's death. Since there
was mail between Israel and the United States, and between the
U.S. and Lebanon, he sent a letter with the sad news to his
brother Elie in New York. Elie wrote a note to a cousin in Beirut
so he could give the word to my grandmother in person.

My father recalls getting the news from my mother's
cousin Izzy Shamah, who had become a close friend.
"When my father died," Dad said, "I was living in Washington and was on a business trip to New York. Elie and I
were in this country. At the hotel room, I got a phone call
from Izzy Shamah, telling me that my father had died. How
long it was after he passed away before I was told, I don't
know. It was a custom in the community not to mention
when somebody died; it was considered to be bad luck. I
was very sad on the telephone, and in fact, I returned to
Washington the same day or next." He and my mother's
relatives went to the synagogue to say *kaddish,* the prayer
for the dead, and observed *shivah,* the traditional Jewish pe-

> **With no
> mail service
> between Israel
> and Lebanon,
> Joe could not
> notify his
> mother directly
> of her hus-
> band's death.**

Selim Sutton, father of eight children, so beloved, respected, and admired within his community, died alone, with none of his family or loved ones around him, and was buried in a cemetery outside Tel Aviv.

riod of mourning. Close friends of my parents and grand-parents came to pay their respects.

Elie visited his father's grave in a cemetery in Petach Tikvah, a suburb of Tel Aviv, on a trip to Israel in 1967. "What I saw saddened me beyond words," he wrote. "I touched the tiny tombstone inscribed with my father's name and date of death; nothing more was written on it. No date of birth. No epitaph. Unsettled, I stared. . . . This was my father, a good man who devoted his life to his family. 'There is no man I love more than you,' I whispered, hoping my words would somehow reach him. For several moments I stood there frozen. None of us had the chance to fulfill our duties to him, to eulogize him, to give him a proper funeral and a proper burial. None of us sat *shivah* for him [at the customary time just after the death]. . . . My fa-ther did so much for us, yet we could not do right by him in death. Heart-wrenching memories will plague me all my life."

My father collects his words with awe and admiration for his own father's strength and foresight.

"I would say that he had a clear insight into the future to do what he did. When your children are teen-agers and you have been an influence in their lives, to make them take a trip to the other side of the world, where—no doubt, in your mind, you know you may not get to see them again . . . ." His voice trailed off.

"You see, I don't believe he was thinking of coming to the United States, any more than any one of the children thought of going back to Syria. He had a lot of chances to come to the United States, which, for some reason, he did not take advantage of. Two of his brothers changed their own future by coming to the United States and raising a family here. My father obviously chose not to come here with them but to stay in Aleppo with his own business. For some reason, he preferred that. He was not in business with his two older brothers, the ones who lost their business in Syria and then moved to Palestine, and he did not want to rely on being with his two younger brothers, who chose to come to the United States. I can't say for sure what his intentions were; I can only base my conclusion on what has really happened, what he did. That's why I never thought he would wind up coming to the U.S., after I left and my brothers left."

Asked what he would say if he could to the father he had not seen since he was a teen, Dad said, "I would want to tell him how right was his thinking, seeing to it that all his children left, because he saw that there was not a bright future for any of them in Syria. He knew to expose us to other countries where the future, as it turned out, is infinitely better than what would have been had they remained in Syria."

Asked what he would say if he could to the father he had not seen since he was a teen, Dad said, "I would want to tell him how right was his thinking."

ॐ

After his father died, Joe had no need to remain in Israel and made plans to return to his mother and brothers in Lebanon. Margo chose to stay in Israel. She had met a man named Nissim Mizrahi, a Sephardic Jew from Morocco, and they were becoming serious about one another. Joe preferred to return to Beirut, as he knew his identity ultimately lay not with the new state of Israel but with his Syrian community.

What Joe discovered, however, was that getting out of Israel was not as easy as getting there had been.

"Going to Israel," he explained, "they welcomed you with open arms. Leaving was another matter entirely. The Israelis did not want you to leave, and the Lebanese did not want to accept you."

Through the grapevine, Joe found someone to smuggle him across the border, but the man, as Joe tactfully recalled, "was not very professional." Israeli guards spotted the group of six Jews as they got close to the border with Lebanon. "Make believe we're picnicking," the smuggler said—a questionable activity for men carrying suitcases with personal belongings over the mountains!

The border guards took them back to town and locked them up. They had a trial before a judge. The smuggler was sentenced to a year in jail. The migrants got thirty days.

"My first week was miserable," Joe recalled of the jail where most of the other prisoners were Arabs arrested for serious crimes. The guards then moved him to a nicer facility, close to Tel Aviv—not really a jail at all, he explained, so much as a place designed to foster an Israeli identity, a means to forge Israeli citizens out of people who had tried to leave. He shared a room with six or seven other men who had meals together, exercised, and did various jobs during the day. They were repeatedly asked to admit that the smuggler had coerced them into trying to leave, but he refused.

"And believe it or not," Joe said with his jovial laugh, "I served my thirty days in jail and I came out."

He got his job back at the nursing home in Tel Aviv and worked there for several more months. Unable to communicate with his family back in Beirut, he maintained contact with Elie and my father in New York, who helped him financially. (To this day there is no mail service between Lebanon

> "Going to Israel," Joe explained, "they welcomed you with open arms. Leaving was another matter entirely.

and Israel.) Joe had friends and a social life in Tel Aviv and enjoyed living there, but he knew he was not going to stay. First, he said, he knew he did not want to serve in the Israeli army, which would have been mandatory if he stayed in Israel. No one of draft age was allowed to leave the country without giving the army two and a half years of military service. If he *had* been willing to serve in the army, he would then have been free to leave—though not to go back to Lebanon or any other Arab country that did not recognize Israel.

But along with not wishing to serve in the military, Joe explained, he knew that his primary connection was with his family. "I was trying to see where my future was going to be. I knew it wasn't going to be in Israel." So after two years in Israel, he attempted to cross the border again.

Joe could not let slip that he was planning to cross the border illegally, so he did not tell any of his friends or co-workers, or even close up his apartment. The only person he told was his sister, Margo. Looking back, he said he was not truly afraid because he was so focused on getting back to Beirut—though he admitted being apprehensive hiking through the mountains in the middle of the night, particularly after having been caught once already. "You know when you have an aim?" he asked gently. "Well, my aim, my objective, was to get to my next destination, back to my family."

On this second attempt, a temperate night in April of 1954, a hired smuggler guided a group of about ten people who had not met one another until that evening. Joe had saved a long time for this passage and paid the smuggler in advance. They left Tel Aviv in the early evening and drove four hours north to the Lebanese border. Everyone wore black clothing so as not to be seen walking all night. Since passage across the border was strictly forbidden, there were no roads, not even a dirt trail, but the smuggler knew just where to take them through the trees so they could cross without being spotted. If they heard anyone or saw a light, they were to drop down immediately and lie on the ground. At one point, someone took out a cigarette and almost lit it

> **On this second attempt to leave Israel, a temperate night in April of 1954, a hired smuggler guided a group of about ten people who had not met one another until that evening.**

before the smuggler grabbed it from his hands. "I thought he was going to kill him!" Joe laughed.

When they reached the Lebanese border the next morning, they were met by other members of the smuggling ring, who dressed them in Arab clothing and put them on buses to Beirut. Joe boarded with the busload of Arabs, disguised as one of them.

Since he could have no direct contact with his family in Beirut while he lived in Israel, his mother had no idea he was coming. He walked in the apartment one afternoon to find his mother and his brother Morris in the kitchen. "I just walked in on them. It was a shock to them," Joe said, again with his good-spirited laugh. "Every time I think about the past, I laugh."

"I have to tell you," he added, shifting to a serious tone. "Your grandma must have been a very, very strong woman, because you see, from beginning to end, the minute the boys got to be 17, 18, 19, she realized she might never see them again. Your father left for China [in 1941], and the first time she saw him after that was in 1957, when she came to America. Uncle Elie left a few years after, and that was the [next] time she saw him. When they were leaving, she had no idea if she was going to see them or not."

His mother might not have known details of their whereabouts or circumstances and yet, "Somehow, somehow, news seeps in, especially bad news. So if they did not hear anything to the contrary, they assumed everything was OK."

☙

Gainfully employed, married to an American citizen, my father at last had his application for permanent residency approved by the U.S. Citizenship and Immigration Office. To complete the legal residency process, the law required that he be interviewed by a consular official in another country and then return to the United States, even if only a few hours later.

"Just crossing the border and returning was all that was required. So I chose to go to Canada for a day. I sent the

> "I have to tell you," Joe added, shifting to a serious tone. "Your grandma must have been a very, very strong woman."

At long last, my dad became a U.S. citizen, receiving his Certificate of Naturalization on November 8, 1956.

necessary papers to the United States Consulate in Toronto for final approval."

Again, more easily said than done.

"I received a letter from the U.S. Consul General in Toronto requiring me to send him either a valid passport or a birth certificate," Dad recalled. "He included a copy of the list of documents for me to send him in order to process the necessary papers. The copy he sent me, though, clearly stated that no birth certificates were issued, nor records kept, for people born in Syria prior to 1932. Since no records of my birth were kept by a government agency, I was in no position to supply him with a birth certificate. And the Syrian passport I carried had expired years before, as the Syrian consulate refused to renew it.

"At that point a great deal of correspondence was exchanged between the U.S. consul general in Toronto and myself. Each time, he made the same requests—namely a valid passport or a birth certificate—and each time, I would advise him of my inability to supply him with these requirements. He would write me, I would write back, he would write back.

"Finally after a few years and a pile of correspondence, he consented for me to come to Toronto and return with the proper documents. You see, before you leave the United States for Canada, they would issue you a reentry permit so you don't go there and get stuck. When I entered his office, he pulls my file and he looks at the file and it's about two inches thick. And he says, you sure write a lot of letters. And I say, 'Sir, you sure would think me awful rude if I didn't answer each letter you wrote me, wouldn't you?'"

Dad returned from Canada as a legal resident, and completed the citizenship process with an exam, which he took in Baltimore in November 1956. Two good friends accompanied him to serve as witnesses to the citizenship oath. These American-born men confided they could not have answered many of the questions on the specifics of our government, constitution, and history.

One by one or in pairs, the rest of the family left Beirut for New York.

CB

One by one or in pairs, the rest of the family left Beirut for New York. They obviously could not procure passports from the Syrian government, which did not even let Jews leave the country. Word got around in Beirut's Jewish community, however, that an official in the Iranian consulate—"who liked money," as Joe said—was selling Iranian passports, in the names of people who had died, to anyone who made some claim of Persian ancestry and paid a hefty fee. Ralph concocted a story about his Persian background and came up with enough money to satisfy the Iranian official.

He arrived in New York in 1955, with his black market Iranian passport and a transit visa for a stop in the United States en route to Mexico. ("All my brothers came here on types of visas that are nonexistent now because of 9/11," my father noted. "Today these things would be much, much harder to arrange.") Ralph settled in the Brooklyn community and found work. Dad by this time was living in Washington. Every six months, as the transit visa came up for renewal, Ralph would go to Washington and my father would accompany him to the Iranian consulate for an extension. Eventually, however, they encountered an official who was wise to the matter. "Oh, really?" he asked Ralph, looking at his Iranian passport. "How much Farsi do you know?" Dad and Ralph left without renewing the visa. My fathers' brothers all knew that they would have to marry American women to get their citizenship. (Most of the family members arrived in New York not knowing a word of English.)

My father's brother Morris followed several months later, with a passport from the same Iranian official who had helped Ralph, and finally my grandmother came with Joe in 1957. Margo and her husband had three children in Israel and moved to New York together in 1972, with help from her brothers.

Edgar, the youngest son, died of kidney failure in 1955 in Beirut at the age of 14. Joe was living there at the time. Ralph, who had just come to America, did not learn of Edgar's death until some time later and was shocked to learn of the death of a brother he remembered as a vibrant, joyous boy. Photos show a glowing young face with a delightful, impish smile.

For the children of Selim Sutton, the paths from the streets of Aleppo had led across decades and continents, through ordeals and success, to happiness for most but an end for others far short of that.

For the children of Selim Sutton, the paths from the streets of Aleppo had led across decades and continents, through ordeals and success, to happiness for most but an end for others far short of that. In the end, their father's foresight, pursued through political upheaval, health crises, religious turmoil, and war, has been rewarded by the productive, healthy, joyous, and religiously free lives of now four generations of descendants. His determination, and that of thousands of men and women like him, has contributed to the vibrancy of Syrian-Jewish communities around the world that maintain the distinct qualities that defined them, as their populations expand far past their size back in Syria. I did not have the good fortune to know this strong, wise, and loving man, but I am indebted to his dream.

Epilogue: Into the Future

yria officially opened its borders for its Jewish citizens in 1992, when President Hafez al-Assad lifted the ban on emigration by Jews and allowed them to leave legally for the first time in forty-four years.

Los Angeles Times reporter Kim Murphy wrote from Damascus in May of that year about the choice facing the forty-five hundred who were left. "Syrian Jews face dilemma: Stay or go," the headline read.

> In the land of Israel's worst enemy, they are one of the oldest Jewish communities in the world. Their ancient synagogues languish along the banks of the Euphrates River, and the sound of their prayers can be heard on the old cobbled streets near the tomb of the Islamic warrior Saladin.
>
> Their kosher butchers stand quietly next to mosques. Goldsmiths with the traditional yarmulkes on their heads bicycle past posters of Syrian President Hafez Assad, his presidential face beaming next to a bouquet of missiles and fighter planes.
>
> Four decades after Syria declared war on Israel, the Jewish quarter here, a neighborhood of 22 synagogues, tiny tailor shops, kosher groceries, and gracious old homes, is one of the most thriving in Damascus. Its inhabitants are largely unrecognizable from other Damascenes except for the identity cards

In 1992, President Hafez al-Assad lifted the ban on emigration by Jews and allowed them to leave legally for the first time in forty-four years.

they carry, stamped "mussawi"—follower of Moses.

But now, bowing to years of pressure from world-wide Jewish organizations who called Syria a prison for its Jews, a new communiqué from Assad permits Syrian Jews for the first time to leave the country without restrictions. The decision has plunged the 4,000-member community—one of the most substantial in the Arab world—into a crisis.

After the horrors of the 1967 Arab-Israeli war, when angry Muslims were allowed unchecked access to the streets of the Jewish quarter, and the years after, when Jews were prohibited from venturing outside the capital and jailed if they went to Israel or attempted to leave the country illegally, the Jews of Syria again are a prosperous, relatively free community.

But they wonder: Is now the time to leave everything they have built and strike out for a new life in America or Israel? With the troubled political climate in the Middle East, many fear that if they do not leave now, the door may be shut again—this time forever. Whole families are being split by the debate: Stay or go.

"It's the chance of a lifetime, but we don't know how long it's going to last," said one young merchant. "For our family, leaving would be a disaster. Where else could we have a life like we have here? But the community depends on each other. If everyone else goes, how can we stay?"

> In the end, "everyone else" went. In 1948, some thirty thousand Jews lived in the Syrian cities of Aleppo, Damascus, and Qamishli. By 2003, fewer than a hundred lived in the entire country.

In the end, "everyone else" went. In 1948, some thirty thousand Jews lived in the Syrian cities of Aleppo, Damascus, and Qamishli. By 2003, fewer than a hundred lived in the entire country. The only functioning synagogue was in Damascus, which once had twenty temples but now did not have enough Jews for a full-time rabbi.

Similar situations have occurred throughout the Muslim

world. The Jewish Virtual Library's "Fact Sheet: Jewish Refugees from Arab Countries" estimates that in 1945, roughly a million Jews lived throughout Algeria, Egypt, Iraq, Lebanon, Libya, Morocco, Syria, Tunisia, and Yemen. In the years after the creation of Israel in 1948, almost all of them fled or were expelled, leaving just seventy-five hundred Jews throughout these countries today, most of them in communities whose residents were too few or too elderly to be sustainable.

This means that for every one of the stories I have gathered of my father and his family, there are literally hundreds of thousands of others. Yet with no Jews still living in these countries to anchor this history and add new chapters to it, their experiences are being forgotten.

The overriding tendency of these Jews of the Arab diaspora has been to move on and not look back. Indeed, the tendency of Jews throughout history has been to carry their identity with them and not have it defined by place. (We say, "Next year in Jerusalem" at the Passover seder, but until 1948, it was simply a metaphor for reconnecting with our Jewish essence within.) Yet something in human nature longs to revisit where we lived, learned, and played when we were young. My father, who for most of my life never voiced a murmur of nostalgia for his birthplace, is no exception.

This means that for every one of the stories I have gathered of my father and his family, there are literally hundreds of thousands of others.

☙

In late summer of 2000, my father's brother Joe and his wife, Eileen, visited Aleppo on a trip to Syria and Lebanon that they took with Joe's brother Ralph and his wife, Sondra. (Ralph and Sondra chose not to accompany them to Aleppo.) Careful to conceal their identity as Jews, Joe and Eileen visited the Suttons' old neighborhood. They found the family's home, boarded up but otherwise just as it had been when they left fifty years earlier. After the lease that Ralph arranged with the Muslim sheikh before he left the country expired, the Syrian government confiscated the house and padlocked it. Joe and Eileen walked past the old synagogue, which no longer had a congregation to serve. Initially fearful of revealing that they were Jewish, Joe was pleasantly surprised on his visit to the Middle East to be well-received by the Muslims. The trip satisfied a deeper urge than he had realized to revisit important places in his past. In Lebanon on that same trip, Ralph visited the grave of his youngest brother, Edgar, in Beirut. He tried to find the apartment they had lived in after leaving Aleppo, but couldn't.

Joe's stories and photos inspired my father's own wish to revisit the town of his childhood.

"Every time I looked at those pictures my brother Joe brought back," Dad said, "I wondered what it would be like to stand on that porch and look in the windows, or just imagine what was inside.

"Before that, I really didn't have any reason to go back. After I arrived in this country, I spent many years getting my residency and United States passport, and I was tied up with living daily life. And I knew that at no time since my family left did we have any family members there. My friends in Aleppo had all gone to other countries: South America, Greece, Italy, Mexico, England, the United States. Now I wanted to see the area I grew up in, walk around the old neighborhood, and see what happened to it since. I would see the synagogue where I spent a lot of years studying and praying, and the house, and the field where we flew kites and played soccer."

Finding the right time proved a challenge. In September 2000, just a few weeks after Joe and Eileen's trip, the second Palestinian Intifada erupted in Israel, inflaming relations between Jews and Muslims throughout the region for years. The 9/11 attacks and wars in Iraq and Afghanistan gave us new trepidation about being American Jewish tourists in a Muslim country. But by 2010, life in Syria seemed sufficiently stable (and our schedules sufficiently open) for my parents and me to begin planning a trip.

Mom, who had never lived in Syria, felt apprehensive about traveling to a country where she might not be wanted,

Joe's stories and photos inspired my father's own wish to revisit the town of his childhood.

My Uncle Joe at the front door of the Sutton home in Aleppo, boarded and padlocked, 2000.

but Dad was eager. We began arranging a trip to Istanbul and Aleppo for April 2011.

In March of that year, however, violence erupted between President Bashar al-Assad's government and rebel forces, and we suspended our plans. For Syrians, the Arab Spring movement that brought hope for democracy throughout the Middle East has devolved into a long, dark winter that shows no signs of abating. As of September 2013, the United Nations estimated at least a hundred thousand Syrian deaths, at least 2 million refugees into neighboring countries, and over 4.25 million more people within the country who have been displaced from their homes by the fighting.

Dad and three of his brothers, from left, Joe, Elie, and Ralph, 2001.

The ongoing conflict and my parents' ages mean my father most likely will revisit his birthplace only in memories, and his family will experience it with him only through stories.

☙

Perhaps the most unexpected twist in the tale is that the end of Jews in Syria has by no means meant the end of Syrian Jews. They have relocated and proliferated around the world, in communities far more populous and financially successful than they were in Syria at their prime. Over seventy-five thousand Syrian Jews live in Brooklyn alone, in a community with its own schools, groceries, businesses, restaurants, synagogues, recreation facilities, senior centers, and cemeteries. (To members of this community, the term "Syrian Jew" includes Jews from Lebanon, Jordan, and Egypt living within the Syrian neighborhoods.)

Other cities in the United States, the United Kingdom, Mexico, Italy, Argentina, Brazil, Chile, Colombia, and Panama also enjoy vibrant, close-knit Syrian communities, whose affiliation with the actual country of Syria is nonexistent. What defines these people as Syrian are the things their families brought with them: religious practices, household traditions, foods, familial bonds, and tenacity. Everything else could be replaced.

Though far fewer in America than the Ashkenazi Jews from Europe and Russia, the Syrian Jews, in their more-compact communities, remain far more tight-knit, religious, and resistant to assimilation.

"Today, if you came to Brooklyn, you would not know that you were not in Syria, except for the language," my father's brother Joe told me recently. "The same foods, the same prayers, the same habits—however it was over there, most of the people are carrying the same traditions here."

Why such loyalty, while other American Jews are relaxing their cultural links, dropping their religious practices, and marrying outside the faith? Perhaps the challenge of being a small sub-minority of Jews in America heightens the urge to protect their distinct identity. This insular life may just be part of the cultural personality of the community, which lived this way even back in Aleppo. Initially ostracized by the Ashkenazi for their Old World customs, Arabic tongue, and different pronunciation of Hebrew prayers, the Syrians today take clear pride in their separateness.

Such clannishness can seem antiquated, oppressive, even comical here in the New World, but it serves as a successful bulwark against disappearance. (When one of my mother's cousins became friends as a young girl with an Ashkenazi Jewish girl, her mother was aghast: "She doesn't know *kibbeh!* She doesn't know *hamud!*"—What could you possibly have in common?) The tenacity of this heritage, several generations after leaving Aleppo, honors the vision of my grandparents, parents, and so many others for whom we descendants feel thanks, love, and awe.

> "Today, if you came to Brooklyn, you would not know that you were not in Syria, except for the language," my father's brother Joe told me recently.

Bibliography

"The Aleppo Codex," *The Aleppo Codex Online. www.alep pocodex.org.*

Bard, Mitchell. "The Jews of Syria." *Jewish Virtual Library.*

Bard, Mitchell. "The Palestinian Refugees." *Jewish Virtual Library.*

Bergman, Ronen. "A High Holy Whodunit." *New York Times Magazine,* July 29, 2012.

"Fact Sheet: Jewish Refugees From Arab Countries." *Jewish Virtual Library.* American-Israeli Cooperative Enterprise, September 2012.

Friedman, Matti. *The Aleppo Codex: A True Story of Obsession, Faith, and the Pursuit of an Ancient Bible.* Chapel Hill, NC: Algonquin of Chapel Hill, 2012.

Gerber, Jane S. *The Jews of Spain: A History of the Sephardic Experience.* New York: Free Press, 1992.

Kranzler, David, and Abraham G. Duker. *Japanese, Nazis, and Jews: The Jewish Refugee Community of Shanghai, 1938–45.* New York: Yeshiva University Press, 1976.

The Last Refuge. Xiao-hong Cheng, director. Ergo Media Inc., 2003. DVD.

Marcus, Abraham. "Aleppo: Post-Medieval," in Encyclopedia of Jews in the Islamic World, Vol. 1. Boston: Brill Academic Publishers, 2010.

Menocal, Maria Rosa. *The Ornament of the World: How Mus-*

lims, Jews, and Christians Created a Culture of Tolerance in Medieval Spain. Boston: Little, Brown, 2002.

The Port of Last Resort. Joan Grossman and Paul Rosdy, directors. 1998.

Roffé, Sarina. "The Jews of Aleppo." Jewish Virtual Library. JewishGen Homepage, Sephardic SIF Homepage.

Sabato, Haim. Aleppo Tales: A Tapestry of Tradition and Faith. New Milford, Conn., Toby Press, 2004.

Shanghai Ghetto. Amir Mann and Dana Janklowicz-Mann, directors. New Video Group, 2005. DVD.

Simarski, Lynn. "The Lure of Aleppo." Saudi Aramco World, July–August. 1987.

Stillman, Norman A. The Jews of Arab Lands: A History and Source Book. Philadelphia, Jewish Publication Society of America, 1979.

"Sugihara: Conspiracy of Kindness, An Interview with David Kranzler." PBS, 1998.

Sutton, Rabbi David, editor, Aleppo, City of Scholars, Brooklyn, NY: Mesorah Publications, 2005.

Sutton, Elie, and Bahia Abrams. Alien at Home: Divine Intervention. New York: Sutco Publishing, 2011.

Sutton, Joseph A.D., Aleppo Chronicles: The Story of the Unique Sephardeem of the Ancient Near East—in Their Own Words. New York: Thayer-Jacoby, 1988.

Murphy, Kim "Syrian Regime Presents Jews With Crisis: Leave or Stay?" Los Angeles Times, May 26, 1992.

Tawil, Hayim, and Bernard Schneider. Crown of Aleppo: The Mystery of the Oldest Hebrew Bible Codex. Philadelphia: Jewish Publication Society, 2010.

Tolan, Sandy. The Lemon Tree: An Arab, a Jew, and the Heart of the Middle East. New York: Bloomsbury Publishing, 2006.

Tuttle, Robert. "The Jews of Syria." SyriaComment.com.

Photo Credits

Page 17, Sephardic Pizminim Project,
http://www.pizmonim.org/overview.php?section=Shuls

Page 18–19, Aleppo Codex Online,
http://www.aleppocodex.org

Page 20, Details from the *Wedding of Ferdinand and Isabella,* artist unknown, 15th century, currently located at the Convento de Las Agustinas, Avila, Spain

Page 21, Wikipedia,
http://en.wikipedia.org/wiki/File:Beyazid_II.jpg

Page 22, *Encyclopedia Judaica,* based on map by H. Bainart.

Page 32–33, Copyright © 2011, Craig Jenkins

Page 35, Reuters

Page 44, Sephardic Pizminim Project,
http://www.pizmonim.org/overview.php?section=Shuls

Page 55, Hulton Archive/Getty Images

Page 63, Navi e Armatori,
http://www.naviearmatori.net/eng/foto-53081-4.html

Page 64, Wikimedia,
http://commons.wikimedia.org/wiki/File:Port_Said_1930s_02.jpg

Page 71, Leo Baeck Institute, http://www.lbi.org/2012/05/
destination-shanghai-exhibit/#2

Page 73, http://img.chinasmack.com/www/wp-content/
uploads/2013/09/historical-shanghai-photos-
early-20th-century-11-1930s.jpg

Page 82, The Tauber Holocaust Library and Education Program online, http://www.tauberholocaustlibrary.org/
archimages/arons19882035/4livingquarters.jpg

Page 94, Wikipedia, http://upload.wikimedia.org/wikipedia/
commons/9/9f/Surrender_of_American_troops_
at_Corregidor%2C_Philippine_Islands%2C_05-
1942_-_NARA_-_535553.jpg

Page 97, Vantage Shanghai online, http://www.vantage-
shanghai.com/highlife/perspectives/2013/01/
shanghais-jewish-community.html/attachment/
hongkou-jewish-6

Page 103, Virtual Shanghai, http://www.virtualshanghai.net/
Asset/Preview/dbImage_ID-198_No-1.jpeg

Page 104, Virtual Shanghai, http://www.virtualshanghai.net/
Asset/Preview/dbImage_ID-2095_No-1.jpeg

About the Author

 laudette E. Sutton is the editor and publisher of *Tumbleweeds*, an award-winning quarterly newspaper for families, which she created in 1995.

She has been a writer and editor since her early years as a teen-ager, with work appearing both in local and national publications and online. For five years she wrote the popular "Family Cafe" column for the *Santa Fe New Mexican*.

Throughout Claudette's career, family has been a major focus, as it is with this book, *Farewell, Aleppo*. In the close-knit community of Syrian Jews that her family was a part of, grandparents, aunts, uncles, cousins, as well as parents and siblings, all helped shape her childhood and mold the driving forces of her professional life. Later, as a young mother in Santa Fe, it seemed only natural for Claudette to think in terms of a similar kind of close support as a venue for applying her journalism training and experience.

This was the beginning of what is now *Tumbleweeds*, a local publication that has been constantly expanding its role in serving Santa Fe's families for almost twenty years. As the quarterly newspaper has grown, so have its scope and community contributions, mixing news, commentary, personal writing, advice, and activity guides—all reflecting Claudette's vision of a powerful resource to help her neighbors face the challenges of parenting.

That start as an editor and publisher arose out of the need she saw back in 1991 as her three-year-old son was entering preschool. The answer was *The Tot's Hot News*, filled with events, articles, listings, and services aimed at parents just like herself. And as both Ariel and the newsletter grew, it morphed into the broader *Tumbleweeds* publication, which has been aimed ever since at families with children of all ages.

Claudette's writing began opening a door to the world for her as a teen-ager. Being a reporter, she realized early, "you can learn about everything"—a much more appealing option after high school than the enforced specialization of college.

After four years at the *Montgomery County Sentinel* in Maryland, the big city beckoned, and Claudette moved to New York, where she earned a general liberal arts degree at the New School and immersed herself more deeply in another side of her extensive family, bringing her closer to the Jewish exodus from Syria that now has formed the backdrop for the story she tells so movingly in *Farewell, Aleppo*.

Claudette and her husband, Charles Brunn, live in Santa Fe, and have one son.

Discussion Guide for Book Groups

1. Claudette Sutton writes: "My father's seemingly simple request to get his story on paper launched questions in my own mind about identity, family, and culture: what remains, what evolves, and what is left behind." To what extent, and in what ways, do you feel that the experiences of prior generations of your family have shaped your identity and values?

2. *Farewell, Aleppo* explores themes of being an insider and outsider, of belonging and not belonging. How do you experience being an insider and an outsider in your family and culture?

3. Claudette's father goes by several names throughout his life: "Miro," "Meïr," "Mike," and briefly "China Mike." Discuss how these different names changed his sense of self.

4. Children in the Syrian-Jewish community are named after their grandparents, in a strictly prescribed order. How does this tradition shape the children's sense of identity and belonging?

5. Mike Sutton describes himself as devoutly observant of Orthodox Jewish laws while growing up in Aleppo—never thinking, for instance, of riding the trolley on the Sabbath or eating non-kosher food, but once he was liv-

ing alone in Shanghai, "Little by little it wore off." What is the catalyst for this disconnection? Is there more than one factor at work?

6. Do you think you would have adapted similarly to Mike in his circumstances, or would you have kept up your religious practices on your own?

7. To what extent do you feel that cultural or religious practices are dependent on our environment and community, and how much are they motivated from within?

8. Certainly, Mike Sutton experienced events whose life-altering nature he could not foresee at the time. Describe a similar kind of circumstance in your own life.

9. The author describes a wistful urge to be a part of her New York family, rather than a benevolent outsider, but feels it would be impossible to absorb herself into such a tight-knit community after growing up in a mainstream America that prized independence and individuality. Do you agree that one needs to grow up in a close-knit community to live by its rules, or is it possible to blend into such a community as an adult?

10. The immigrant experience of Syrian Jews in America has differed dramatically from that of other ethnic groups in terms of how fiercely they have resisted assimilation. Why do you think the Syrian Jews have been inclined, and able, to adhere so closely to their centuries-old traditions and values?

11. Some people feel strongly that their identity was shaped by the physical environment they grew up in, whether a natural landscape or an urban setting. Others feel their identity was determined not by place but by personal or familial choice. How do you feel?

12. Which do you value more in your own life, assimilation into the nation's culture or adherence to your cultural background? Discuss the advantages and disadvantages of each.

13. What did you know about the Shanghai Jews before reading this book?

14. What did you know about the Jews of Middle Eastern countries before reading this book? How has this book changed your understanding of Jewish and Arab relationships historically?

15. Aleppo is very much in the news these days, as civil war ravages Syria and millions of people are displaced from their homes. What role, if any, do you feel the outside world should play in supporting the Syrian people during this conflict? And how would supporting the Syrian people differ from supporting the Syrian government?

Made in the USA
San Bernardino, CA
12 March 2016